NC STATE

DAILY
DEVOTIONS
FOR
DIE-HARD
FANS

WOLFPACK

NC STATE

Daily Devotions for Die-Hard Fans: NC State Wolfpack
© 2010 Ed McMinn

Library of Congress Cataloging-in-Publication Data
13 ISBN Digit ISBN: 978-0-9840847-4-6

Manufactured in the United States of America.

For bulk purchases or to request the author for speaking engagements, email contact@extrapointpublishers.com.

Go to http://www.die-hardfans.com for information about other titles in the series.

Cover and interior design by Slynn McMinn.
Edited by Walter E. Harrison III

TABLE OF CONTENTS

DAY 1

IN THE BEGINNING

Read Genesis 1, 2:1-3.

"God saw all that he had made, and it was very good" (v. 1:31).

The Farmers and Mechanics of the North Carolina State College of Agricultural and Mechanical Arts went undefeated in their initial football season. It helped that they played only one game.

The football program at what would be NC State began in 1892 when a group of students petitioned the board of trustees for $50 to field a team. Money wasn't the only obstacle the A&M boys had to overcome to get the program started. The school received some federal funds that came with a catch: All physically fit students in the all-male student body had to attend military drills three days a week unless the faculty excused them. Since no lighted fields were available, arranging practice time was a serious problem. Though faculty members wrestled with the concept of intercollegiate athletics -- which had already begun at the universities of North Carolina and Virginia -- the instructors made collegiate football possible by excusing the members of the football team from drills so they could practice.

Unlike most schools, A&M had some students who knew something about this newfangled game that was sweeping across the nation's college campuses. Intramural football had begun with the school's birth in 1889. Students and nonstudents alike had taken part in a club football team in 1890 and '91.

Bart Gatling was the coach of the first three A&M teams. The first game was played on March 12, 1892, at what is now Pullen Park before about 200 spectators. In pink and blue uniforms (red and white did not appear until 1895), the Aggies whipped Raleigh Male Academy 14-6 in the season's lone game.

College football was in Raleigh to stay. In 1893, the school's second team also went undefeated with wins over Tennessee and those same Raleigh Academy males.

Beginnings are important, but what we make of them is even more important. Consider, for example, just how far the NC State football program has come since that first season.

Every morning, you get a gift from God: a new beginning. God hands to you as an expression of divine love a new day full of promise and the chance to right the wrongs in your life. You can use the day to pay a debt, start a new relationship, replace a burned-out light bulb, tell your family you love them, chase a dream, solve a nagging problem . . . or not.

God simply provides the gift. How you use it is up to you. People often talk wistfully about starting over or making a new beginning. God gives you the chance with the dawning of every new day. You have the chance today to make things right – and that includes your relationship with God.

The most important key to achieving great success is to decide upon your goal and launch, get started, take action, move.
                                                        -- John Wooden

Every day is not just a dawn; it is
a precious chance to start over or begin anew.

DAY 2

THE PIONEER SPIRIT

Read Luke 5:1-11.

"So they pulled their boats up on shore, left everything and followed him" (v. 11).

What would have been the first basketball game in NC State history was in effect rained out.

Two students were the primary pioneering force that brought basketball to North Carolina A&M. In a much more innocent and simpler time, athletics at the school was largely a student matter. The students paid athletic association dues of $6, and a group of elected student officers basically ran the association.

Wake Forest began playing basketball in 1905, and North Carolina tipped off for the first time in 1910. In response to student interest at A&M, the association in 1910 appointed Guy K. Bryan, a senior from Tampa, to head up a committee to investigate the feasibility of starting a team at the school. Percy Bell Ferebee, a junior from Elizabeth City, N.C., who became captain of the first team, was his right-hand man. Student support for a team came quickly. So did basketball.

The first game was set for Thanksgiving Day in 1910 against Virginia Tech in Norfolk prior to the football game. But since A&M had no gymnasium on campus, the team had to practice outside. A series of heavy rains washed out most of the practices, and the game was cancelled.

Team manager W.H. Davis then scheduled two games against

Wake Forest. The first-ever A&M game was played at the Wake gym on Feb. 16, 1911. The results were predictable as the more experienced Wake men blew past the Raleigh guys 33-6.

In the second meeting, played in Pullen Hall, Coach E.V. Freeman's "Farmers" took advantage of a floor that was rendered slick by a dance the night before to surprise Wake Forest 19-18.

Going to a place in your life you've never been before requires a willingness to take risks and face uncertainty head-on. You may have never helped start a new sports program at a major college, but you've had your moments when your latent pioneer spirit manifested itself. That time you changed careers, ran a marathon, volunteered at a homeless shelter, learned Spanish, or went back to school.

While attempting new things invariably begets apprehension, the truth is that when life becomes too comfortable and too familiar, it gets boring. The same is true of God, who is downright dangerous because he calls us to be anything but comfortable as we serve him. He summons us to continuously blaze new trails in our faith life, to follow him no matter what. Stepping out on faith is risky all right, but the reward is a life of accomplishment, adventure, and joy that cannot be equaled anywhere else.

The names of G.K. Bryan and P.B. Ferebee will stand out as the pioneers on the frontier of [basketball] at their Alma Mater.
-- The Red & White in 1911

**Unsafe and downright dangerous, God calls us
out of the place where we are comfortable to a life
of adventure and trailblazing in his name.**

DAY 3

STRANGE BUT TRUE

Read Isaiah 9:2-7.

"The zeal of the Lord Almighty will accomplish this" (v. 7).

Strange but true: The coach who basically created ACC basketball never played the game.

Everett Norris Case loved basketball. Closer to the truth is that basketball consumed him. It was said of him, "He had no family, and few other serious interests. He simply wanted to spread the word about the greatest game ever invented." Fortunately for the Wolfpack, NC State gave him the chance, and in 1946, he came to Raleigh "to start a new legend and a new religion."

Money didn't lure Case from Indiana. He accepted the head coaching job without ever seeing the campus and refused to talk about salary. "That's not important," he said. "Money isn't the big consideration." What did lure him was "the hulking skeleton of steel that would later become Reynolds Coliseum. Case saw it as an opportunity to make Raleigh 'The Basketball Capital of the World.'" That meant doing something few Southern schools bothered with: creating "a whole basketball program that involved recruiting, coaching and promoting."

Case's success in Raleigh forced UNC to hire Frank McGuire to keep up. Duke hired Case assistant Vic Bubas to catch up. "Carolina and Duke and the others [the ACC schools] were forced to improve (because of Case)," Jim Valvano once said.

WOLFPACK

Case changed the game on Tobacco Road forever. He introduced the Indiana tradition of cutting down the nets, he was the first coach in the area to have summer camps, and he devised the box score that shows player stats. And he won. He won more high school state championships than anybody in Indiana history at the time. Then, in 17 seasons at State before bad health forced his retirement in 1964, he was 377-134 with ten conference championships. And it's strange but it's true: He never played the game.

Life is just strange, isn't it? How else to explain the college bowl situation, Dr. Phil, tattoos, curling, tofu, and teenagers? Isn't it strange that today we have more ways to stay in touch with each other yet are losing the intimacy of personal contact?

And how strange is God's plan to save us? Think a minute about what God did. He could have come roaring down, destroying and blasting everyone whose sinfulness offended him, which, of course, is pretty much all of us. Then he could have brushed off his hands, nodded the divine head, and left a scorched planet in his wake. All in a day's work.

Instead, God came up with a totally novel plan: He would save the world by becoming a human being, letting himself be humiliated, tortured, and killed, and thus establishing a kingdom of justice and righteousness that will last forever.

It's a strange way to save the world – but it's true.

He is the one who brought basketball to the ACC.
-- John Wooden on Everett Case

It's strange but true: God allowed himself
to be killed on a cross to save the world.

DAY 4

A SURE THING

Read Romans 8:28-30.

"We know that in all things God works for the good of those who love him, who have been called according to his purpose" (v. 28).

That Scott Wood could shoot was a sure thing, but the Wolfpack got more than that in the deal.

Wood was practically born shooting. When he was 2, his dad, who played for Western Carolina, took him to a basketball booth at the state fair. The kind of booth with the undersized rims and over-inflated basketballs. The younger Wood's career as a shooter was born a stuffed animal prize later. "I didn't care about the prize," Wood said. "I just wanted to shoot."

When Wood turned 5, he was already taking 500 shots a day on a 10-foot rim. By the time he entered high school, his reputation as a gunner was spreading. State assistant coach Monte Towe visited Marion, Ind., just to watch him shoot in an empty gym before practice. "He hit about every shot he took," Scott's dad recalled. "Maybe 75 straight free throws and . . . 30 3-pointers."

When Wood finally arrived in Raleigh in the fall of 2009, he was already being called State's best pure shooter since Rodney Monroe (1988-91). Wood knew what everyone was expecting to see; he also knew what they would get. "I knew I'd come and surprise people because I figured they would think I was just some slow, white farm kid," he said.

WOLFPACK

Oh, State got its shooter, all right. On Jan. 12, 2010, he poured in 31 points in an 88-81 win over FSU. But the Pack also got a player whose defensive skills were a revelation, a player with such a complete game that coach Sidney Lowe called him a "throwback." He started all 36 games at small forward in 2009-10 and hit 63 treys, the second-highest total ever for a State freshman.

Basketball games aren't played on paper. That is, you attend a State game expecting the Pack to win, but you don't know for sure they will, just as Scott Wood doesn't know for sure that he'll hit his next shot. If you knew they'd win, why bother to go? Any game worth watching carries with it an element of uncertainty.

Life doesn't get played on paper either, which means that living, too, comes laden with uncertainty. You never know what's going to happen tomorrow or even an hour from now. Oh, sure, you think you know. For instance, right now you may be certain that you'll be at work Monday morning or that you'll have a job next month. Life's uncertainties, though, can intervene at any time and disrupt your nice, pat expectations.

Ironically, while you can't know for sure about this afternoon, you can know for certain about forever. Eternity is a sure thing because it's in God's hands. Your unwavering faith and God's sure promises lock in a certain future for you.

There is nothing in life so uncertain as a sure thing.
-- NHL coach Scotty Bowman

**Life is unpredictable and tomorrow is uncertain;
only eternity is a sure thing
because God controls it.**

DAY 5

MAKE NO MISTAKES

Read Mark 14:66-72.

"Then Peter remembered the word Jesus had spoken to him: 'Before the rooster crows twice you will disown me three times.' And he broke down and wept" (v. 72).

Lorenzo Charles' mistake turned into one of the most famous moments in collegiate sports history.

The experts saw a mismatch in the NCAA finals of April 4, 1983, as the Wolfpack met the high-flying Phi-Slamma-Jamma of Houston. Jim Valvano, however, used senior point guard Sidney Lowe to control the tempo and negate Houston's fearsome fast break. Lowe played what amounted to a perfect game; he was on the court for all forty minutes with eight points, five steals, eight assists, and not a single turnover.

Thus, State kept hanging around, trailing only 52-46 with 3:19 left. Lowe hit and then senior guard Dereck Whittenburg nailed a pair of 20 footers to tie the game with 1:59 on the clock. Valvano ordered an intentional foul, Houston missed, and State ran the clock down to 44 seconds before calling a time out.

Valvano wanted his team to hold the ball down to ten seconds whereupon Lowe would penetrate and create a shot. Houston, however, refused to cooperate, using an aggressive zone defense that nearly forced a turnover and threw the whole State offense into a state bordering on panic.

Trapped in the corner, senior forward Thurl Bailey managed to get a pass to Whittenburg, who stood thirty feet from the basket with time running out. He threw up a 29-foot prayer that Charles answered by grabbing the air ball and dunking it at the buzzer.

The sophomore forward should never have been where he was. "I was . . . exactly where you don't want to be if you are going to be a decent offensive rebounder," Charles said.

But it was the mistake that won a national championship.

It's distressing but it's true: Like basketball players and Simon Peter, we all make mistakes. Only one perfect man ever walked on this earth, and no one of us is he. Some mistakes are just dumb. Like locking yourself out of your car or falling into a swimming pool with your clothes on. Other mistakes are more significant. Like heading down a path to addiction. Committing a crime. Walking out on a spouse and the children.

All these mistakes, however, from the momentarily annoying to the life-altering tragic, share one aspect: They can all be forgiven in Christ. Other folks may not forgive us; we may not even forgive ourselves. But God will forgive us when we call upon him in Jesus' name.

Thus, the twofold fatal mistake we can make is ignoring the fact that we will die one day and subsequently ignoring the fact that Jesus is the only way to shun Hell and enter Heaven. We absolutely must get this one right.

I was in the wrong place at the right time.
                                    -- Lorenzo Charles on his famous rebound

**Only one mistake we make sends us to Hell
when we die: ignoring Jesus while we live.**

DAY 6

FAMILY TIES

Read Mark 3:31-35.

"[Jesus] said, 'Here are my mother and my brothers! Whoever does God's will is my brother and sister and mother'" (vv. 34-35).

For the Buckey boys, even a college choice was about family. As a result, State landed two record setters for its football team.

Dave and Don Buckey admitted they visited Raleigh in 1972 because they had never ridden on an airplane before. The twins from Akron, Ohio, weren't really the right size for major college football anyhow. They were only six feet tall with Don the heavier by ten pounds at 177.

"We had decided to go to college together," Dave said. "Most of the schools we heard from were from the Mid-American Conference." The only major college that contacted them was somewhat confusing. Purdue made a weak try with a letter from assistant coach Bo Rein. Then two weeks later they got another letter from Rein -- recruiting them for NC. State. They had to conduct a little research to find out that Rein had changed schools.

But that second letter from Rein intrigued the duo with the possibility that State was seriously interested in them. So -- quite literally to go along for the ride -- they flew to Raleigh. "Don and I were just going down to N.C. State to take the trip, to get our first airplane ride," Dave said. The trip became something more, however. They really liked head coach Lou Holtz and the students

WOLFPACK

they met. "The other colleges we had visited had not shown much school pride, but the people at State had a lot of it," Dave said. The clincher came when Holtz charmed the rest of the Buckey family. For the Buckeys, this was a family decision.

With a two-for-one deal, State landed the greatest pass-and-catch combo in school history until that time. From 1972-75, quarterback Dave set a school record with 4,286 career yards while wide receiver Don set Pack records with 102 catches for 1,735 yards.

Some wit said families are like fudge, mostly sweet with a few nuts. You can probably call the names of your sweetest relatives, whom you cherish, and of the nutty ones too, whom you mostly try to avoid at a family reunion.

Like it or not, you have a family, and that's God's doing. God cherishes the family so much that he chose to live in one as a son, a brother, and a cousin.

One of Jesus' more startling actions was to redefine the family. No longer is it a single household of blood relatives or even a clan or a tribe. Jesus' family is the result not of an accident of birth but rather a conscious choice. All those who do God's will are members of Jesus' family.

What a startling and wonderful thought! You have family members out there you don't even know who stand ready to love you just because you're part of God's family.

We did everything together, and, yes, we really did admire each other.
-- Don Buckey on his relationship with twin brother Dave

**For followers of Jesus, family comes not from
a shared ancestry but from a shared faith.**

DAY 7

NOISEMAKER

Read Psalm 100.

"Shout for joy to the Lord, all the earth!" (v. 1)

The crowd noise totally confused a pair of NC State basketball players. In response, they combined to produce one of the Wolfpack's biggest field goals ever.

In the 2002 ACC Tournament, the fourth-seeded Pack smashed Virginia 92-72 in the quarterfinals and then met top-seeded and second-ranked Maryland in the semis. The Terps had beaten them twice during the regular season in "rugged, gritty contests."

The game unfolded as a series of streaks. The Pack led 24-12 after ten minutes; Maryland rallied with a 19-2 run; State came back with a 17-6 run to lead 79-66 with 3:56 left. But the Terrapins had one last streak in them and closed to 81-78 with 1:53 left.

State went into its spread offense, which had frustrated the Terps before by producing backdoor layups and open jumpers. This time, though, the Maryland defense played tough, and State wound up with nothing but a bunch of passes as the shot clock wound down.

Since the game was played on a "neutral" floor in Charlotte, the crowd noise was constant. Freshman Ilian Evtimov wound up with the ball, and he heard the crowd counting down: "5, 4, 3, . . " He said to himself, "Hold on, I thought we had about 15 seconds left." So he quickly fired a pass to freshman Julius Hodge, who also heard the crowd noise and was also confused by it. "I was thinking, 'Is that the Maryland fans, or ours?'" He made a decision. "I figured it was ours and that I better get the shot off, quick."

So Hodge let fire with a 22-foot jumper from the right wing that hit the net just as the shot-clock buzzer went off. The desperate 3-pointer made it 84-78 State with 1:17 to play. The Terps couldn't recover; State won 86-82 and was on its way to the league tourney finals and eventually the NCAA Tournament. Thanks in part to a little confusion because of the crowd noise.

Whether you're at a State game live or watching on TV, no doubt you've contributed to the crowd noise generated by thousands of fans or just your buddies. You've probably been known to whoop it up pretty good at some other times in your life, too. The birth of your first child. The concert of your favorite band. That fishing trip when you caught that big ole bass.

But how many times have you ever let loose with a powerful shout to God in celebration of his love for you? Though God certainly deserves it, he doesn't require that you walk around waving pompoms and shouting "Yay, God!" He isn't particularly interested in having you arrested as a public menace.

No, God doesn't seek a big show or a spectacle. A nice little "thank you" is sufficient when it's delivered straight from the heart and comes bearing joy. That kind of noise carries all the way to Heaven; God hears it even if nobody else does.

Southern football fans are knowledgeable, fair -- and loud.
-- Broadcaster George Mooney

The noise God likes to hear is a heartfelt
"thank you," even when it's whispered.

WEATHERPROOFED

Read Nahum 1:3-9.

"His way is in the whirlwind and the storm, and clouds are the dust of his feet" (v. 3b).

Paul Horvath wasn't the least bit interested in playing college basketball, especially at NC State. Then the weather got hot.

Horvath was a 6-6 native of Chicago who never played high school ball. He got his first taste of the game while he was serving with the army in Europe during World War II. His teammates included future Wolfpack players Jack McComas and Vic Bubas. When coach Everett Case told his 1946-47 squad he was looking for a center and a guard, McComas recommended his army buddies. Case set his sights on Horvath, who turned out to be an extremely reluctant recruit.

Horvath had returned to Chicago after the war and had started technical school to study electronics. He received a letter from Case in the spring of 1947. "They were having a tryout somewhere in Indiana, and he wanted me to come over," Horvath recalled. So what did he do about the opportunity? "I wasn't really interested in going to college, so I just balled the letter up and threw it out."

Case sent Horvath another letter inviting him to call anytime for a visit and a tryout. Horvath didn't toss that letter, but he did stuff it into a drawer and pretty much forgot about it.

By this time, he had quit technical school and was learning welding. "I thought I had found my life's work," he said. But then something happened: It got hot early in Chicago that summer. Suddenly, college basketball in Raleigh was a lot more appealing.

Horvath called Case, flew to Raleigh on a weekend, and spent a few minutes passing and shooting with forward Ed Bartels. Case said come on down and play; Horvath did.

The player driven to basketball by the weather started all four seasons (1948-51 -- 111 wins) and as a senior was second-team All-Southern Conference and a unanimous choice for team MVP.

A thunderstorm washes away your golf game or the picnic with the kids. Lightning knocks out the electricity just as you settle in at the computer. A tornado interrupts your Sunday dinner and sends everyone scurrying to the hallway. A hurricane blows away your beach trip.

For all our technology and our knowledge, we are still at the mercy of the weather, able only to get a little more advance warning than in the past. The weather answers only to God. Rain and hail will fall where they want to.

We stand mute before the awesome power of the weather, but we should be even more awestruck at the power of the one who controls it, a power beyond our imagining. Neither, however, can we imagine the depths of God's love for us, a love that drove him to die on a cross for us.

It wasn't long before I realized that I hadn't found my life's work.
-- Paul Horvath on the heat that changed his mind about welding

**The power of the one who controls the weather is
beyond anything we can imagine,
but so is his love for us.**

DAY 9

NEVER TOO LATE

Read Genesis 21:1-7.

"And [Sarah] added, 'Who would have said to Abraham that Sarah would nurse children? Yet I have borne him a son in his old age'" (v. 7).

David Thompson had a plan that included getting his college degree. It just took him almost thirty years to do it.

"David Thompson is the greatest player ever in college basketball." That blunt assessment came from an opponent, Len Elmore, an All-America at Maryland. Thompson's teammate and friend Tommy Burleson agrees, offended that the ACC in 2003 named Michael Jordan and not Thompson its greatest athlete ever.

Basketball's legendary Skywalker was a three-time ACC Player of the Year (1973-75) who led NC State to an undefeated season in 1973 and the national title in 1974. In 1975, he set the school record by averaging 29.9 points per game and still owns the State record for highest career scoring average (26.8 ppg).

Thompson ended his career at State with a technical foul and a standing ovation at the same time. The dunk was illegal in college ball when Thompson played, but late in his final home game, he got loose on a breakaway and slammed the dunk home. Coach Norm Sloan took him out immediately after that. "It was a great way to end my career," Thompson said.

But he didn't end his academic career as greatly. He left State in the spring of 1975 two electives short of earning his degree in sociology. Finally, when he watched his daughters working on their degrees, he decided he had to beat them to it. He enrolled in summer school in 2003 and walked across a stage that December.

Not surprisingly, Thompson's home is filled with many of the awards and honors resulting from his basketball life. Still, "the diploma is something I am more proud of," he said. "It's just a feeling of completion, that's all. It completes me."

Even if it did take more than twenty-eight years.

Getting that college degree. Getting married. Starting a new career. Though we may make all kinds of excuses, it's often never too late for life-changing decisions and milestones.

This is especially true in our faith life, which is based on God's promises. Abraham was 100 and Sarah was 90 when their first child was born. They were old folks even by the Bible's standards at the dawn of history. But God had promised them a child and just as God always does, he kept his promise no matter how unlikely it seemed.

God has made us all a promise of new life and hope through Jesus Christ. At any time in our lives – today even -- we can regret the things we have done wrong and the way we have lived, ask God in Jesus' name to forgive us for them, and discover a new way of living – forever.

It's never too late to change. God promised.

It was something that bothered me for a lot of years.
-- David Thompson on not having his college degree

It's never too late to change a life
by turning it over to Jesus.

DAY 10

LESSON LEARNED

Read Psalm 143.

"Teach me to do your will, for you are my God" (v. 10).

Kellie Harper learned a lesson. The wisdom she gained changed the way she prepared her team for the 2010-11 season.

In April 2009, Harper was named the third-ever head coach of the NC State women's basketball team. She inherited a squad that the pundits picked to finish ninth in the league. Instead, they won twenty games, advanced to the finals of the league tournament, and landed in the NCAA Tournament. Marissa Kastanek was the ACC Freshman of the Year; soph Bonae Holston was honorable mention All-ACC.

Harper's first year with the Wolfpack and the ACC was, not surprisingly, one big learning experience. For instance, she said, she learned that her players were both resilient and young women of character. She learned they were competitive.

Those were certainly nice things to learn, but as the season wore on, Harper saw something that wasn't so good: Her team was not nearly as big nor as strong as most of the opposition. That first problem could be solved through recruiting "or some kind of medieval stretching device," but most likely her team wasn't going to be much taller for the 2010-11 season.

That other situation, however, could be addressed -- at once. So at 6.a.m, shortly after the first-round loss to UCLA in the NCAA Tournament, Harper had her team at work -- in the weight room in the most intense workouts of their young lives.

"You can tell it's helping a lot," said junior guard Emili Tasler. "I feel like my arms are bulging. I've hurt a couple of people by accident, just trying to work hard."

"You have to be strong," Harper declared about navigating and surviving the grind of the ACC season. Lesson learned.

Learning about anything in life requires a combination of education and experience. Education is the accumulation of facts that we call knowledge; experience is the acquisition of wisdom and discernment, which add purpose and understanding to our knowledge.

The most difficult way to learn is trial and error: dive in blindly and mess up. The best way to learn is through example coupled with a set of instructions: Someone has gone ahead to show you the way and has written down all the information you need to follow.

In teaching us the way to live godly lives, God chose the latter method. He set down in his book the habits, actions, and attitudes that make for a way of life in accordance with his wishes. He also sent us Jesus to explain and to illustrate.

God teaches us not just how to exist but how to live. We just need to be attentive students.

We want to be the team that other teams are scared to play because we're more physical than they are.
— Wolfpack guard Emili Tasler on the team's weightlifting program

To learn from Jesus is to learn what life is all about and how God means for us to live it.

NC STATE

DAY 11

WORK ETHIC

Read Matthew 9:35-38.

"Then he said to his disciples, 'The harvest is plentiful but the workers are few. Ask the Lord of the harvest, therefore, to send out workers into his harvest field'" (vv. 37-38).

When Everett Case took the head coaching job at NC State in 1946, he immediately went to work bringing basketball not just to the university but to the whole state.

At the time, basketball was played so little and so poorly in North Carolina that for his first team, Case returned to his native Indiana and recruited ten players. Even as late as 1950, he did not have a single North Carolinian among his starters.

As soon as he lined up his first recruiting class, Case turned his attention to promoting basketball in the state. He and assistant coach Carl "Butter" Anderson gave clinics across North Carolina, talking basketball and NC State. "We made speeches at all the schools in the state trying to get them new gyms," Anderson recalled. The coaches worked through Ruritan Clubs, Kiwanis Clubs, and other groups. Anderson especially liked the Ruritan Clubs because they always gave the coaches a ham when they visited. "Our idea was to get the gyms built and to let the game grow so we could recruit in the state," Anderson said.

Asked once at Madison Square Garden in New York City about the absence of players from North Carolina on his team, Case was insightful and honest. He replied that everyone knew the best players were in states such as Indiana and New York, and he used players from those states to form teams that would increase interest in North Carolina. "Everywhere you go now, you find youngsters imitating these players," Case said. "Now, when you travel around the state, you see hoops hung on pine trees and backboards and baskets on almost every vacant lot."

The coaches' hard work paid off. Before long -- and to this day -- basketball was and is the state's No. 1 sport.

Do you embrace hard work or try to avoid it? No matter how hard you may try, you really can't escape hard work. Funny thing about all these labor-saving devices like cell phones and laptop computers: You're working longer and harder than ever. For many of us, our work defines us perhaps more than any other aspect of our lives. But there's a workforce you're a part of that doesn't show up in any Labor Department statistics or any IRS records.

You're part of God's staff; God has a specific job that only you can do for him. It's often referred to as a "calling," but it amounts to your serving God where there is a need in the way that best suits your God-given abilities and talents

You should stand ready to work for God all the time, 24-7. Those are awful hours, but the benefits are out of this world.

You have to have an enthusiasm for life. You have to have a dream, a goal, and you have to be willing to work for it.
— Jim Valvano

**God calls you to work for him using the talents
and gifts he gave you; whether you're a worker
or a malingerer is up to you.**

DAY 12

FOR ALL YOU KNOW

Read John 8:12-32.

"You will know the truth, and the truth will set you free"
(v. 32).

The Wolfpack players and coaches knew they were going to the 1983 NCAA Tournament, where they would be playing, and whom they would be playing. They just had no clue where the site of their game was.

"If we had lost [to Wake Forest] today, we wouldn't have a shot at the NCAA," declared senior guard Sidney Lowe. But the Pack didn't lose. Lorenzo Charles' free throw with three seconds left gave State a 71-70 win over Wake Forest in the opening round of the 1983 ACC Tournament in Atlanta.

Coach Jim Valvano had it figured the same way. Virginia, UNC, and Maryland were in the 52-team field, the coach believed; the fourth ACC team would be the winner of the State-Wake game. Pencil State in. After that, it became a matter of positioning, getting the best possible pairing for the Wolfpack. Oh, and winning the tournament, too, which State did, beating North Carolina 91-84 and Virginia 81-78.

The team was still in Atlanta when it gathered to watch ESPN for the tournament pairings. When "No. 6 seed NC State" flashed on the screen, everybody shouted. But then came total befuddlement. Their opponent was Pepperdine -- in Corvallis. No one even knew where either Pepperdine or Corvallis was. The trainer, Jim

WOLFPACK

Rehbock, who had to make the travel arrangments, thought Corvallis was in California. Assistant coach Ed McLean ventured a suggestion that it might be in Oregon. Valvano had no idea. When Thurl Bailey called the hotel desk and asked where Corvallis was, the reply was a question: "Is that somewhere in Atlanta?"

Nobody knew where Corvallis was, but they managed to get there and begin the run to the national championship.

There's much you just flat don't know. Maybe it's the formula for the area of a cylinder, where Corvallis is (Oregon), or the capital of Myanmar. You may not know how paper is made from trees. Or how toothpaste gets into the tube. And can you honestly say you know how the opposite sex thinks?

Despite your ignorance about certain subjects, you manage quite well because what you don't know generally doesn't hurt you too much. In certain aspects of your life, though, ignorance is anything but harmless. Imagine, for instance, the consequence of not knowing how to do your job. Or of getting behind the wheel without knowing how to drive a car.

In your faith life, what you don't know can have awful, eternal consequences. To willfully choose not to know Jesus is to be condemned to an eternity apart from God. When it comes to Jesus, knowing the truth sets you free; ignoring the truth enslaves you.

My sister's expecting a baby, and I don't know if I'll be an uncle or an aunt.

— NBA player Chuck Nevitt

**What you don't know may not hurt you
except when it comes to Jesus.**

DAY 13

A BETTER PLACE

Read Hebrews 11:13-16.

"They were longing for a better country — a heavenly one" (v. 16a).

Kay Yow coached for 34 years at NC State, but she finally found a better place.

The Hall of Fame women's basketball coach died on Jan. 24, 2009, after an inspiring battle against breast cancer. Yow was a coaching legend whose 737 wins made her the fifth all-time winningest coach in women's basketball history.

When she was hired at State in 1975, taking over a program that barely existed, the job didn't pay much, but she did get a car in the deal. She gave her old one to her mother. She coached State into the big time: four ACC Tournament championships, twenty appearances in the NCAA Tournament, and a Final Four in 1998. She also coached the U.S. women's team to gold medals at the 1988 Seoul Olympics. In 2002, she was the fifth women's coach inducted into the Naismith Basketball Hall of Fame.

It was, however, what Yow was rather than what she did that so endeared her, not just to State fans, but to admirers all over the country. As UConn head coach Geno Auriemma put it, "Everyone feels a connection with Kay. She's a competitor, but she's a great human being, first and foremost." Her life was a blessing to those who were fortunate enough to know her.

Especially in the Wolfpack nation did her death hit hard. State

coach Carter Jordan tearfully spoke of his team of wrestlers being visibly upset upon learning of her death.

So how could this "beacon of hope and determination and love and joy" find a better place after she was blessed to spend most of her life at NC State, which is about as good as it gets? Again, it comes back to what she was. "First and foremost she was a Christian," said one who knew her. That explains much. Kay Yow loved Jesus Christ enough to make him the Lord of her life. And so she has indeed found a better place -- with him.

America is a nation of nomads, packing up the U-Haul and the car and moving on the average about once every five years. We move because we're seeking something better. Better schools for the kids. A job with better career opportunities. Better weather.

We're seeking that better place that will make our lives better. Quite often, though, we wind up in a place or in circumstances that are just different, not better. So we try again.

God is very aware of this deep longing in our hearts for something better than what we have now. As only he can, he has made provision for it. What God has prepared for us, however, isn't a place that's just better, but rather a place that is perfect. He has also thoughtfully provided clear directions about how to get there, though we won't get any help from our GPS.

Jesus is the way to that place, that perfect place called Heaven.

I know she's in a better place, [but] I'm going to miss her.
-- A friend of Kay Yow's upon her death

God knows our deep longing for a better place,
so he has prepared one for us: Heaven.

NC STATE

EXCUSES, EXCUSES

Read Luke 9:57-62.

"Another said, 'I will follow you, Lord; but first let me go back and say good-by to my family'" (v. 61).

Fans generally don't put a lot of stock into excuses for a lousy year. For three seasons in the 1940s, though, NC State's basketball team had an excuse everyone could accept: Its best players were in the Army.

While World War II drastically altered the landscape of college athletics across the country, State was hit a good bit harder than most. What first-year Red Terror coach Leroy Jay saw when he surveyed his team for 1943-44 was total devastation. Only one of the eleven lettermen from the 15-7 team of 1941-42 was back.

The carnage wasn't due solely to graduation, but rather to a set of circumstances that left State at an extreme competitive disadvantage. State was an officer training ground for the U.S. Army, which alone of the military services did not allow its trainees to participate in collegiate athletics. This meant that the experienced athletes -- including some formerly at NC State -- were now suiting up for North Carolina with its Marine program or Duke with its Navy training program.

What Jay had left were 16- and 17-year old freshmen and men who did not qualify for military service. Wake Forest found itself with a similar predicament and finally gave up, not bothering to field a basketball team in 1944-45.

WOLFPACK

The football situation was so lopsided that State didn't play Duke in football in 1944 or UNC for three seasons. Jay and his basketball program played on, though the records weren't anything to brag about. The Red Terrors went 5-13 in 1943-44, 10-11 in 1944-45, and 6-12 in 1945-46. During those three seasons, State lost all fifteen of its games against UNC and Duke.

But they had a quite valid excuse: For the most part it was boys against men, and some of the men were former State players.

Has some of your most creative thinking involved excuses for not going in to work? Have you discovered that an unintended benefit of computers is that you can always blame them for the destruction of all your hard work? Don't you manage to stammer or stutter some justification when a state trooper pulls you over? We're usually pretty good at making excuses to cover our failures or to get out of something we don't particularly want to do.

That holds true for our faith life also. The Bible is too hard to understand so I won't read it; the weather's too pretty to be shut up in church; praying in public is embarrassing and I'm not very good at it anyway. The plain truth is, though, that whatever excuses we make for not following Jesus wholeheartedly are not good enough.

Jesus made no excuses to avoid dying for us; we should offer none to avoid living for him.

There are a thousand reasons for failure but not a single excuse.
-- Former NFL player Mike Reid

Try though we might, no excuses can justify
our failure to follow Jesus wholeheartedly.

DAY 15

AS A RULE

Read Luke 5:27-32.

"Why do you eat and drink with tax collectors and 'sinners'?" (v. 30b)

Norm Sloan had a few simple rules for his players that they ignored at their peril. He had nothing but disdain, though, for the NCAA rules that kept him from helping his players.

Sloan was one of Everett Case's legendary "Hoosier Hotshots" of 1946. He coached the Wolfpack from 1966-80, winning 266 games, three ACC titles, and the 1974 national title. He was inducted into the North Carolina Sports Hall of Fame in 1994.

Before each season, he called his players together to explain the rules they had to live by to play basketball at NC State. The rules were simple: "Go to class, trim your hair, tuck in your shirts, have your ankles taped before practice every day and be on time." Sloan went on to say, "If you don't want to do that, then don't worry about it. You don't have to do any of those things." Then came the clincher: "But you have to pay your own way to college and you can't play basketball for me."

So Sloan clearly expected his Wolfpack to abide by his rules. On the other hand, he had no qualms about breaking NCAA rules if a player needed help. In a book, he openly confessed to breaking many rules for his players. He said he gave players who needed it money for trips home or to help their families; he helped Phil Spence's mother buy heart medication she couldn't afford; he

loaned Tommy Burleson $20 for his dorm deposit.

Sloan said he was primarily concerned with "illegal aid," that he never cheated to recruit a player. "But to me," he said, "once a kid gets [to State], he's family" and he should be taken care of, rules or no rules.

You live by rules others set up. Some lender determined the interest rate on your mortgage and your car loan. You work hours and shifts somebody else established. Someone else decided what day your garbage gets picked up and what school district your house is in.

Jesus encountered societal rules also, including a strict set of religious edicts that dictated what company he should keep, what people, in other words, were fit for him to socialize with, talk to, or share a meal with. Jesus ignored the rules, choosing love instead of mindless obedience and demonstrating his disdain for society's rules by mingling with the outcasts, the lowlifes, the poor, and the misfits.

You, too, have to choose when you find yourself in the presence of someone whom society deems undesirable. Will you choose the rules or love? Are you willing to be a rebel for love — as Jesus was for you?

We took a bad lick. It was uncalled for, it was inexcusable, it was laughable compared to what goes on today.
> -- *Norm Sloan on the one-year probation at State*

**Society's rules dictate who is acceptable
and who is not, but love in the name of Jesus
knows no such distinctions.**

DAY 16

HOW WE LEAVE

Read 2 Kings 2:1-12.

"A chariot of fire and horses of fire appeared and separated the two of them, and Elijah went up to heaven in a whirlwind" (v. 11).

Darrion Caldwell did his best to leave NC State, but it just didn't work out. A few months later, he was a national champion.

During the summer of 2008, Caldwell decided the time had come for him to leave Raleigh. "They were not letting me play football. I just thought [this] wasn't for me," the Wolfpack wrestler, a rising junior, said. "I wanted to be back home."

So Caldwell went to his coach, Carter Jordan, seeking a release. Jordan refused. "I knew I was doing what was best for Darrion athletically, socially, academically," Jordan said. Caldwell didn't see it that way; mad at his coach, he set about creating his own way to leave Raleigh, even if leaving meant giving up the sport that had made him one of the top three wrestling prospects in the country in high school. He looked into playing football for Rutgers, which is near his home.

Then during a summer wrestling camp, Jordan invited his disgruntled wrestler to come sit down for a talk. Everything changed. "Basically, it was my waking up and realizing everything I had going for me here," Caldwell said. "There was no reason for me to change." And no reason to leave.

The summer of his discontent behind him, Caldwell returned

to wrestling with a vengeance, accelerating his training regimen that enhanced what Jordan described as Caldwell's "incredible God-given ability." On March 21, 2009, Caldwell etched his name onto the short list of State's all-time greatest athletes. He won the NCAA championship in the 149-pound class by "dismantling" the top-seeded wrestler 11-6 in the finals.

Caldwell had a lot of plans after that, including the Olympics. His plans, however, no longer included leaving NC State early.

Like Darrion Caldwell and Elijah, we can't always choose the exact circumstances under which we leave somewhere.

You probably haven't always chosen the moves you've made in your life. Perhaps your company transferred you. A landlord didn't renew your lease. An elderly parent needed your care.

Sometimes the only choice we have about leaving is the manner in which we go, whether we depart with style and grace or not. Our exit from life is the same way. Unless we usurp God's authority over life and death, we can't choose how we die, just how we handle it. Perhaps the most frustrating aspect of dying is that we have at most very little control over the process. As with our birth, our death is in God's hands. We finally must surrender to his will even if we have spent a lifetime refusing to do so.

We do, however, control our destination. How we leave isn't up to us; where we spend eternity is -- and that depends on our relationship with Jesus.

I'm glad I came back to State. I'm glad I could achieve this here.
-- Darrion Caldwell on his national championship

How you go isn't up to you; where you go is.

DAY 17

THE MOTHER LODE

Read John 19:25-30.

"Near the cross of Jesus stood his mother" (v. 25).

Because he listened to his mother, NC State landed a player who scored one of the most important field goals in school history on the greatest team in school history.

Phil Spence grew up in Raleigh and played one All-American season at junior college. Major-college coaches from all over the country soon came calling. That's when Spence's mother gave her son some sagacious advice. "Why are you going to go all over the world to get something that you can find right in your backyard?" she asked. Spence listened to her and went to State.

As a sophomore on the national championship team of 1973-74, Spence was a part-time starter, sharing time with fellow power forward Tim Stoddard. He averaged 6.4 points and 6.3 boards.

His most important contribution that special season came in the finals of the '74 ACC Tournament, the legendary game with 4th-ranked Maryland. (See Devotion No. 52.) With time ticking away in the overtime, the Terps led 100-99. Point guard Monte Towe spotted Spence open under the basket and hit him with a strike. Spence made a layup with less than 30 seconds left to give State the lead. The Pack won 103-100 in an age when only the winner of the ACC Tournament made it to the NCAA Tournament.

Spence listened to his mama one more time in his college basketball career. He averaged 13.1 points per game for the 22-6 Pack of 1974-75 and led the team with 10.0 rebounds per game. He then applied for hardship entry into the NBA draft; he had 48 hours to change his mind. Maggie Spence was again ready with some words of wisdom for her son. "If you go pro, it's just a matter of time. And time will run out," she said.

He decided to stay in school and averaged 13.9 points and 9.1 boards as a senior. He was drafted by the Milwaukee Bucks.

Mamas often are a fount of wisdom as they face the challenge of steering their children along the right path. No mother in history, though, has faced a challenge to match that of Mary, whom God chose to be the mother of Jesus. Like mamas and their children throughout time, Mary experienced both joy and perplexity in her relationship with her son.

To the end, though, Mary stood by her boy. She followed him all the way to his execution, an act of love and bravery since Jesus was condemned as an enemy of the Roman Empire.

But just as mothers like Mary, Maggie Spence, and maybe even your mom would apparently do anything for their children, so will God do anything out of love for his children. After all, that was God on the cross at the foot of which Mary stood, and he was dying for you, one of his children.

Everyone should find time to write and to go see their mother. I think that's healthy.

— Bear Bryant

**Mamas often sacrifice for their children,
but God, too, will do anything out of love
for his children, including dying on a cross.**

DAY 18

THE GOOD OLD DAYS

Read Psalm 102.

"My days vanish like smoke; . . . but you remain the same, and your years will never end" (vv. 3, 27).

Once upon a time, in the good old days, the Christmas social scene in Raleigh included an event that was even bigger than the ACC Tournament: The Dixie Classic.

The Classic was part of a different time and era in collegiate athletics. It arose out of an evening in 1949 at Coach Everett Case's apartment when Dick Herbert, the sports editor for *The News & Observer*, came up with the idea for a holiday basketball tournament when school was not in session that would involve the four local teams and four of the best teams in the country. Case corralled the eight teams; local response was immediate. More than 54,000 spectators attended the first tournament, and its national reputation grew quickly.

The Classic was a rarity in that it offered schools a chance to make money on basketball. That fact alone ensured the best teams, but the tournament was always about more than money. It became a part of Raleigh's holiday swirl as the community threw what amounted to a Christmas party for the visitors. The visiting teams were formally welcomed at the airport and were the guests of honor at activities that included dinners in town. "The merchants bureau was very involved," remembered C.A. Dillon, longtime Wolfpack public address announcer. "The whole town was involved."

Penn State coach John Egli never forgot the ovation that his star, Jesse Arnelle, received in the 1949 Classic. "I still have a chill down my spine when I remember it," he said. "The fans here appreciate a fine player no matter what team he plays for."

The last Dixie Classic, in 1960, drew a record crowd and paid each team almost $21,000 plus expenses. But a point-shaving scandal at State -- a reminder that even the good old days had a dark side -- and a resulting de-emphasis on basketball made the Classic an easy target. Officials ended it after 1960.

Time just never stands still. The current of your life sweeps you along until you realize one day you've lived long enough to have a past. Part of it you cling to fondly. The stunts you pulled with your high-school buddies. Your first apartment. That dance with your first love. Those "good old days."

You hold on relentlessly to the memory of those old, familiar ways because of the stability they provide in our uncertain world. They will always be there even as times change and you age.

Another constant exists in your life too. God has been a part of every event in your life that created a memory because he was there. He's always there with you; the question is whether you ignore him or make him a part of your day.

A "good old day" is any day shared with God.

A glorious 12-year tradition became a memory.
-- Writer Douglas Herakovich on the end of the Dixie Classic

Today is one of the "good old days"
if you share it with God.

DAY 19

GOAL ORIENTED

Read 1 Peter 1:3-9.

"For you are receiving the goal of your faith, the salvation of your souls" (v. 9).

When he was 17, Jim Valvano wrote down his life's goals. No one knew it at the time, of course, but that short list would lead to one of NC State's most glorious athletic achievements.

Valvano's goals were as lofty as could be expected of a teenager. They didn't, however, mention a wife. In fact, Valvano was so dedicated to sports he didn't even date in high school. When the boyfriend of a certain Pamela Levine went off to college, she put the word out that she wanted to go to the prom. Valvano asked her, even though she had to drive since he didn't have a license. After the prom, the couple went out to dinner, and Pamela ordered lobster tails, which created a small problem: Valvano didn't have enough money to pay for them. He excused himself in mid-meal and placed a panicked phone call to his dad for a bailout. "Dad, I didn't even know lobsters had tails!" he wailed. Pamela Levine, of course, later became Pam Valvano.

Valvano wrote those goals down on a 3x5 index card and wasn't a bit shy about letting folks see them. 1) He would be a starting guard in high school 2) and in college. 3)) He would then become a head college coach, 4) advance to the big time, and 5) win an NCAA championship.

He started for his father, Rocco, at Seaford High in Long

Island. Check. He started for Rutgers and was the Senior Athlete of the Year. Check. Head coaching jobs at Johns Hopkins, Bucknell, and Iona followed. Check. And then it was on to the big-time: NC State. Check.

That meant one goal from that faded index card still remained: the little matter of the national title. To answer any questions or allay any concerns about that one, please refer to the 1982-83 college basketball season. Or ask any Wolfpack fan.

What are your goals for your life? Have you ever thought them out as Jim Valvano did? Or do you just shuffle along living for your paycheck and whatever fun you can seek out instead of pursuing some greater purpose?

Now try this one: What is the goal of your faith life? You go to church to worship God. You read the Bible and study God's word to learn about God and how God wants you to live. But what is it you hope to achieve? What is all that stuff about? For what purpose do you believe that Jesus Christ is God's son?

The answer is actually quite simple: The goal of your faith life is your salvation, and this is the only goal in life that matters. Nothing you will ever seek is as important or as eternal as getting into Heaven and making sure that everybody you know and love will be there too one day.

If I ever accomplish [a goal], I'll set a higher goal and go after that.
-- Bobby Bowden

**The most important goal of your life
is to get to Heaven and to make sure the folks you
know and love will be there one day too.**

DAY 20

THE GREATEST

Read Mark 9:33-37.

"If anyone wants to be first, he must be the very last, and the servant of all" (v. 35).

Wolfpack senior John Sadri battled to the finish in what more than three decades later is still regarded as the greatest championship match in NCAA men's tennis history.

On a sunny afternoon in Georgia in 1978, Sadri strode onto the tennis courts in Athens decked out in his usual attire: a black five-gallon cowboy hat and a red State blazer. He showed up to take on Stanford freshman John McEnroe for the NCAA singles title. What resulted "was drenched with drama, suspense, and enough tension to almost break [the players'] racquet strings."

Sadri was a two-time All-America who was 55-4 his last two seasons at State. He won two conference singles crowns and two ACC doubles titles and helped State claim two conference team championships. He went on to play ten years as a professional, achieving a world singles ranking of No. 14 in 1980.

That afternoon in Athens he played the greatest match of his college career. The collision of the Johns lasted four hours and 13 minutes. When it was over, McEnroe took the title with a grueling 7-6, 7-6, 5-7, 7-6 triumph that was even closer than the score would indicate. McEnroe won just one more point and one more game than Sadri did. McEnroe won each tiebreaker 5-4; Sadri never lost his serve during the match.

WOLFPACK

Aware of McEnroe's propensity for immature outbursts and Sadri's steely refusal to back down from anyone, officials allowed the head coaches (J.W. Isenhour for State) to sit courtside for the first time ever. Once when McEnroe started showing out, Sadri snapped at him, "Hey, let's play tennis; let's not carry on like that; I'm not going to take this."

So they played, every shot under pressure, every point pivotal in the greatest match in NCAA men's singles history.

We all want to be the greatest. The goal for the Wolfpack and their fans every season is the national championship. The competition at work is to be the most productive sales person on the staff or the Teacher of the Year. In other words, we define being the greatest in terms of the struggle for personal success. It's nothing new; the disciples saw greatness in the same way.

As Jesus illustrated, though, greatness in the Kingdom of God has nothing to do with the world's understanding of success. Rather, the greatest are those who channel their ambition toward the furtherance of Christ's kingdom through love and service, rather than their own advancement, which is a complete reversal of status and values as the world sees them.

After all, who could be greater than the person who has Jesus for a brother and God for a father? And that's every one of us.

[McEnroe] was a great player, [but] I really felt I was going to win.
-- John Sadri

**To be great for God has nothing to do
with personal advancement and everything to do
with the advancement of Christ's kingdom.**

DAY 21

DEAD WRONG

Read Matthew 26:14-16; 27:1-10.

"When Judas, who had betrayed him, saw that Jesus was condemned, he was seized with remorse" (v. 27:3).

No way am I going to take someone that size. He'll get eaten alive in the ACC." Boy, was Norm Sloan wrong.

Sloan was looking for a point guard during the 1970-71 season, and former Pack All-America Dick Dickey recommended one. He urged Sloan to sign an Indiana kid, but when he told the coach the player was only 5'7" tall -- well, that's when Sloan uttered his dead-wrong declaration.

But Dickey reminded the coach how he had once recommended a 6'3" center to him and had been rebuffed because of his size. That player went on to an All-SEC career at Auburn, and Sloan told Dickey that he would take the next player he recommended, sight unseen. Now was the time; that player was Monte Towe.

Even after Towe arrived in Raleigh, the coaches didn't really realize what they had on their hands. "We never thought [Towe] was going to be the player that he was," said Sam Esposito, who served as a Sloan assistant and the head baseball coach.

What really happened was that Towe ate the ACC alive. He was in the starting lineup the moment he became eligible as a sophomore and in the fabled season of 1973-74 was "the heart and soul" of the national champions. He was first-team All-ACC in 1974 and owns the second-highest career scoring average in State history (20.6 ppg).

Towe and David Thompson are generally credited with inventing the "alley oop." In a day when dunks were illegal, Towe was a master at lobbing the ball to Thompson, who would catch it and lay it in without dunking. The first time he saw the play pulled off in practice, Sloan deadpanned, "That's a pretty good play."

He was right about that, just wrong about Towe.

There's wrong, there's dead wrong, and there's Judas wrong. We've all been wrong in our lives, but we can at least honestly ease our conscience by telling ourselves we'll never be as wrong as Judas was. A close examination of Judas' actions, however, reveals that we can indeed replicate in our own lives the mistake Judas made that drove him to suicidal despair.

Judas ultimately regretted his betrayal of our Lord, but his sorrow and remorse, however boundless, could not save him. His attempt to undo his initial wrong was futile because he tried to fix everything himself rather than turning to God in repentance and begging for mercy.

While we can't literally betray Jesus to his enemies as Judas did, we can match Judas' failure in our own lives by not turning to God in Jesus' name and asking for forgiveness for our sins. In that case, we ultimately will be as dead wrong as Judas was.

It was pretty clear that I was No. 7 of seven. I am not even sure I was very close to No. 6.
-- Monte Towe on where he stood on the State freshman team

A sin is the first wrong; failing to ask God for forgiveness of it is the second.

HEART OF THE MATTER

Read 1 Samuel 13:1-14.

"The Lord has sought out a man after his own heart" (v. 14).

Everybody knew UNC had more talent. As it turned out, though, the Wolfpack had more heart -- and that's what made the difference.

On Feb. 3, 2007, 12-8 NC State hosted 20-2, third-ranked North Carolina in what was clearly a mismatch. Heels head coach Roy Williams had not lost a game to the Pack since he took the job; State had a first-year boss in Sidney Lowe. As one writer put it, UNC "smashed the Pack 95-71 at the RBC Center last season, and many believed there could be a repeat this year." They were all wrong. In a glorious night that left the Center floor flooded with red after the final buzzer and had State players high-fiving the likes of heroes such as David Thompson, Tom Burleson, and Chris Corchiani, NC State won 83-79.

State took a 38-36 lead into the halftime dressing room on a drive by junior Gavin Grant that went the length of the floor. The Pack owned the first ten minutes of the last half; they built a 10-point lead that Grant capped off with a reverse, fast-break jam that brought the house door. The biggest lead was 71-60. Carolina never caught up.

The win was no fluke. The Pack outrebounded Carolina 31-25 and controlled the tempo, refusing to let the Heels run. State shot an incredible 75 percent from the field the last half, hitting 13 of 17 shots. Courtney Fells had a career-high 21 points. Sophomore Ben McCauley had 17. Brandon Costner scored 15 and had 11 boards. Grant scored 16. Senior point guard Engin Atsur played with a sore hamstring but still had 12 points and ten assists.

How was all this possible? McCauley knew. "We wanted it more than they did," he said. It turns out this particular win over the Tar Heels was a matter of the heart.

We all face defeat in our lives. Sometimes, even though we fight with all we have, we lose. Even State loses games.

At some time, you probably have admitted you were whipped no matter how much it hurt. Always in your life, though, you have known that you would fight for some things with all your heart and never give them up: your family, your country, your friends, your core beliefs.

God should be on that list too. God seeks men and women who will never turn their back on him because they are people after God's own heart. That is, they will never betray God with their unbelief; they will never lose their childlike trust in God; they will never cease to love God with all their heart.

They are lifetime members of God's team; it's a mighty good one to be on, but it takes heart.

They had more passion for the game than we did and I don't understand that. I'll never understand that.
-- UNC coach Roy Williams after the loss to State

**To be on God's team requires the heart
of a champion.**

DAY 23

IN THE BAD TIMES

Read Philippians 1:3-14.

"What has happened to me has really served to advance the gospel. . . . Because of my chains, most of the brothers in the Lord have been encouraged to speak the word of God more courageously and fearlessly" (vv. 12, 14).

Earle Edwards knew the situation was bad at NC State when he took over the football program in 1954; he just didn't know how bad -- and it wasn't just wins and losses.

Edwards had spent his coaching career at Penn State and Michigan State, where football was popular and supported. In Raleigh, though, at the time, Everett Case's basketball program was king while football "was floundering in mediocrity." Earle found that "playing conditions were poor, training tables for the athletes were not acceptable, recruiting budgets were practically nonexistent, and there was hardly any pride in the football team."

"It was not the fault of anyone, but the conditions were difficult," Edwards later recalled. When he came to NC State, "the total football income -- guarantees, attendance, everything" was only $50,000. Michigan State's was ten times that.

Edwards knew what would solve the problem: good players. The situation at State was so bad, however, that in the early days he couldn't even get the state's most outstanding players to visit, let alone commit. His first year he had enough money to hand out only thirteen scholarships.

In 1957, though, the "Earle of Raleigh" coached the Pack to the ACC championship, the school's first, and a 7-2-1 record. His 1963 squad went to the Liberty Bowl, and his 1967 team went 9-1 and beat Georgia in that same bowl, the school's first-ever bowl win

Edwards had led the program to some good times that included his 9-8 record against archival North Carolina.

Loved ones die. You're downsized. Your biopsy looks cancerous. Your spouse could be having an affair. Hard, tragic times are as much a part of life as breath.

This applies to Christians too. Christianity is not the equivalent of a Get-out-of-Jail-Free card, granting us a lifelong exemption from either the least or the worst pain the world has to offer. While Jesus promises us he will be there to lead us through the valleys, he never promises that we will not enter them.

The question therefore becomes how you handle the bad times. You can buckle to your knees in despair and cry, "Why me?" Or you can hit your knees in prayer and ask, "What do I do with this?"

Setbacks and tragedies are opportunities to reveal and to develop true character and abiding faith. Your faithfulness -- not your skipping merrily along through life without pain -- is what reveals the depth of your love for God.

I always thought I could fix up a football program, but I'll admit I didn't realize how much of a challenge there was at State.
— Earle Edwards

**Faithfulness to God requires faith even in --
especially in -- the bad times.**

DAY 24

BROKEN DREAMS

Read Joel 2:28-32.

"I will pour out my Spirit on all people. . . . Your old men will dream dreams" (v. 28).

Like all young boys, Terry Gannon had his dreams growing up, only his most important one didn't come true -- for which Wolfpack fans are still grateful.

Gannon grew up in Joliet, Ill. His dream through his childhood and into his teen years was the same as every other Irish-Catholic schoolboy in town who played sports. "I went to bed for 12 years praying I could play for Notre Dame," Gannon said. He even had dinner with the real-life Rudy the night after his famous appearance against Georgia Tech and wound up with the helmet Rudy wore in that game.

Gannon's game was basketball, but when he was a senior in high school, he was only six feet tall, though he was his school's all-time leading scorer. Notre Dame head coach Digger Phelps, took one look in Gannon's direction and declared, "He is too small."

Gannon had to put away his broken dream and replace it with a new one. NC State was it.

As a sophomore in 1982-83, Gannon hit 53 of 90 threes for the national champs, a percentage (58.9) that is still the ACC record. When Dereck Whittenburg broke his foot, Gannon was forced to assume a greater role in the offense. He went on to make clutch shots, crucial free throws, and big defensive stops in the run to the title. He was the team's second-leading scorer in 1984; a leg infection slowed him down his senior season. He was the basketball program's first Academic All-America.

Gannon got a little payback for that broken dream. A career in broadcasting put him in the studio with Phelps. He frequently would ask the coach, "Hey, Digger, do you have your ring on?" He then would flash his national title hardware and add, "Oh, that's right, you don't have one."

Like Terry Gannon, we all have particular dreams. Perhaps to make a million dollars, write the Great American Novel or find the perfect spouse. More likely than not, though, we gradually lose our hold on those dreams. They slip away from us as we surrender them to the reality of everyday living.

But we also have general dreams. For world peace. For an end to hunger. That no child should ever again be afraid. These dreams we hold doggedly onto as if something inside us tells us that even though the world gets itself into a bigger mess every year, one day everything will be all right.

That's because it will be. God has promised a time when his spirit will rule the world. Jesus spoke of a time when he will return to claim his kingdom. In that day, our dreams of peace and plenty and the banishment of hate and want will be reality.

Our dreams based on God's promises will come true.

Be a dreamer. If you don't know how to dream, you're dead.
-- Jim Valvano

Dreams based on God's promises will come true.

DAY 25

KEEP OUT

Read Exodus 26:31-35; 30:1-10.

"The curtain will separate the Holy Place from the Most Holy Place" (v. 26:33).

Leo Katkaveck was such an outsider that at first his teammates ignored him and his coach insulted him. He eventually became the ultimate insider, twice the team captain and once the MVP.

Katkaveck was the lone player to play basketball for NC State before and after World War II, lettering in 1942 before he joined the service. After the war, he was leaning toward playing for North Carolina because they had had a great season the year before. When he ran into C.A. Dillon, the longtime public address announcer for Wolfpack football and basketball, Dillon urged Katkaveck to give the new coach a chance and he did.

That new coach was Everett Case. When Katkaveck showed up in Raleigh, the welcome he received wasn't exactly that of a returning hero. He had not played much basketball since being released from the service and admitted that he was "a little out of shape." The first time Katkaveck met his coach, Case looked him over and said "You're kind of tubby, aren't you?"

He met with an even cooler reception from his new teammates. For his first team, the 1946-47 squad, Case recruited ten players from Indiana, the legendary "Hoosier Hotshots." A tight-knit bunch who knew each other and their coach, they simply ignored Katkaveck. "They were all kind of full of themselves," he said.

"But they were nice guys, and once we started winning (They went 26-5 Case's first year.), we were one big, happy family."

Indeed. "Leo was a little older, a little more mature than we were, and he held us together," said All-American Dick Dickey. Case once called Katkaveck "the best guard in the country." The outsider was captain of both the 1947 and 1948 squads and was named the team's MVP after the 1947-48 season.

That civic club with membership by invitation only. The bleachers where you sit while others frolic in the sky boxes. That neighborhood you can't afford a house in. You know all about being shut out of some club, some group, some place. "Exclusive" is the word that keeps you out.

The Hebrew people, too, knew about being told to keep out; only the priests could come into the presence of the holy and survive. Then along came Jesus to kick that barrier down and give us direct access to God.

In the process, though, Jesus created another exclusive club; its members are his followers, Christians, those who believe he is the Son of God and the savior of the world. This club, though, extends a membership invitation to everyone in the whole wide world; no one is excluded. Whether you're in or out depends on your response to Jesus, not on arbitrary gatekeepers.

There are clubs you can't belong to, neighborhoods you can't live in, schools you can't get into, but the roads are always open.
-- Nike

Christianity is an exclusive club, but an invitation is extended to everyone and no one is denied entry.

DAY 26

PAIN RELIEF

Read 2 Corinthians 1:3-7.

"Just as the sufferings of Christ flow over into our lives, so also through Christ our comfort overflows" (v. 5).

Ted Brown knew about playing with pain. The greatest pain he ever played with, however, wasn't physical at all.

Brown is the greatest running back in NC State history. More than three decades after he last wore the red and white as a senior in 1978, Brown is still the school's single-game (251 vs. Penn State in 1977), season (1,350 in 1978), and career (4,602) rushing leader. He remains State's all-time scoring leader with 312 points; his 51 career touchdowns is the school record, and his 49 rushing TDs remain the ACC record. Brown is the only player in ACC history to be named first-team all-conference four times. He was All-America in 1978, ending his career as the fourth leading rusher in NCAA history. He was named an ACC Legend in 2010.

In 1978, Brown was consistently mentioned in preseason hype as a leading candidate for the Heisman Trophy. "We felt Ted's chances for the Heisman were very good," said sports information director Ed Seaman. Through the first five games of the season, Brown had the numbers to put him among the favorites. But then, as Seaman put it, "He got banged up."

Two knee injuries and a shoulder injury slowed Brown down to the point that he didn't start against Maryland, the first time in 35 games he wasn't in the opening lineup. But Brown played in

WOLFPACK

that game as he always played through the pain.

Especially his junior season. The week before the Syracuse game his mother died. At home all week, Brown didn't plan to return for the game until his father talked him into it. He didn't expect to play because team rules forbade it when a player missed practice all week. An exception was made for the circumstances.

Playing with Pain, Brown had a 95-yard touchdown run, the longest in ACC football history. State won 38-0.

Since you live on Earth and not in Heaven, you are forced to play with pain. Whether it's a car wreck that left you shattered, the end of a relationship that left you battered, or a loved one's death that left you tattered -- pain finds you and challenges you to keep going.

While God's word teaches that you will reap what you sow, life also teaches that pain and hardship are not necessarily the result of personal failure. Pain in fact can be one of the tools God uses to mold your character and change your life.

What are you to do when you are hit full-speed by the awful pain that seems to choke the very will to live out of you? Where is your consolation, your comfort, and your help?

In almighty God, whose love will never fail. When life knocks you to your knees, you're closer to God than ever before.

For any running back to be good, he has to play hurt. But it's no fun to be hurt.

-- Ted Brown

**When life hits you with pain, you can always
turn to God for comfort, consolation, and hope.**

THE SUB

Read Galatians 3:10-14.

"Christ redeemed us from the curse of the law by becoming a curse for us" (v. 13).

In 1965, a State sub came off the bench to win the most valuable player trophy at the ACC Tournament.

Larry Worsley was Coach Press Maravich's sixth men on the 1964-65 squad. Early on, Worsley played very little, but when he came off the bench to score six points and spark a comeback win over Clemson, Maravich moved him into the sixth-man slot.

"From that time on, I got real confident," Worsley said. "If we were in a lull and having trouble scoring, [Maravich would] tell me to go in and shoot the ball." In fact, about the only time Worsley got in trouble with his coach was when he passed up open shots. More than once, Maravich told his sub he would bench him if he didn't shoot more.

Worsley's ACC Tournament began with 12 points in a 106-69 rout of Virginia in the opening round. Against Maryland the next night, he scored 15 points in the win. Then in the finals against 8th-ranked Duke, Worsley broke loose. After sitting out the first 15 minutes of the game, he went in and scored a career-high 30 points on 14 of 19 shooting from the floor. State won 91-85.

Duke coach Vic Bubas used a zone defense shifted to Worsley's side, then a man-to-man, and finally a box-and-one, but nothing worked. "It was too much Worsley," the former Everett Case assistant said. "He was the difference."

When the buzzer sounded and Worsley and his teammates were celebrating, Worsley's brother came up and said, "Boy, you're going to be the most valuable player." Worsley laughed it off, but his brother insisted. When the sub thought it over a minute, he said, "Dang, I might be it." He was, the only non-starter ever to win the tournament MVP award.

Wouldn't it be cool if you had a substitute like Larry Worsley for all life's hard stuff? Telling of a death in the family? Call in your sub. Breaking up with your boyfriend? Job interview? Chemistry test? Crucial presentation at work? Let the sub handle it.

We do have such a substitute, but not for the matters of life. Instead, Jesus is our substitute for matters of life and death. Since Jesus has already made it, we don't have to make the sacrifice God demands for forgiveness and salvation.

One of the ironies of our age is that many people desperately grope for a substitute for Jesus. Mysticism, human philosophies such as Scientology, false religions such as Hinduism and Islam, cults, New Age approaches that preach self-fulfillment without responsibility or accountability – they and others like them are all pitiful, inadequate substitutes for Jesus.

Accept no substitutes. It's Jesus or nothing.

I never had any idea how many points I had scored or anything. I just knew we won. That's all I cared about.
– Larry Worsley after the win over Duke

**There is no substitute for Jesus,
the consummate substitute.**

DAY 28

A SECOND CHANCE

Read John 7:53-8:11.

"'Then neither do I condemn you,' Jesus declared. 'Go now and leave your life of sin'" (v. 8:11).

On nothing but a desperate coach's hunch, Jay Davis received a second chance. And NC State got a win.

Davis was the starting quarterback for the Wolfpack against Wake Forest on Oct. 2, 2004. He lasted only two series, hitting 3-of-6 passes for a paltry 19 yards. Coaches benched him in favor of redshirt freshman Marcus Stone, who played the rest of the half. At the break, the Pack trailed 14-0, and the offense had done little to help out as Davis sat on the bench. "I was not upset at all," he said. "I consider myself a team player, and I just wanted to win the football game."

When the Pack hit the field for the second half, offensive coordinator Noel Mazzone turned to the junior QB and said simply, "Jay, you're in." Given a second chance, Davis didn't waste it. On his fourth play, he hit flanker Sterling Hicks down the right sideline for a 57-yard touchdown bomb. "One play sparked it all," head coach Chuck Amato said about the score.

On the first play of State's next series, after a 40-yard touchdown pass to Richard Washington was nullified by a penalty, Davis hit halfback Tramain Hall open over the middle. He rambled 58 yards to the Wake 3; tailback T.A. McLendon scored from there. The Pack then grabbed the lead on the next series, driving 66 yards, capped by freshman tailback Bobby Washington's 2-yard sweep.

State led 21-14. Wake did manage to get it together long enough to tie the game with 8:08 left and send it into overtime. After the Deacs missed a field goal, McLendon carried four straight times, the last an 8-yard rumble up the middle. State won 27-21.

"At halftime I would have started you [at quarterback]," Mazzone told a reporter after the game. But he had a hunch and gave Davis a second chance. Davis finished the day with 228 yards passing, one touchdown toss, and no interceptions.

"If I just had a second chance, I know I could make it work out." Ever said that? If only you could go back and tell your dad one last time you love him, take that job you passed up rather than relocate, or replace those angry shouts at your son with gentle encouragement. If only you had a second chance, a mulligan.

As the story of Jesus' encounter with the adulterous woman illustrates, with God you always get a second chance. No matter how many mistakes you make, God will never give up on you. Nothing you can do puts you beyond God's saving power. You always have a second chance because with God your future is not determined by your past or who you used to be. It is determined by your relationship with God through Jesus Christ.

God is ready and willing to give you a second chance – or a third chance or a fourth chance – if you will give him a chance.

We were looking for anything to spark us.
-- State coach Noel Mazzone on putting Davis back into the game

You get a second chance with God
if you give him a chance.

DAY 29

JUST PERFECT

Read Matthew 5:43-48.

"Be perfect, therefore, as your heavenly Father is perfect"
(v. 48).

State softball coach Lisa Navas was bewildered by all the fuss her team was making over pitcher Abbie Sims. It wasn't like her senior ace hadn't thrown a shutout or a no-hitter before. Ah, but this one was different; this one was perfect.

Sims is the greatest pitcher in State softball history. She finished her Wolfpack career in 2007 with school records that included lowest career ERA (1.69), lowest opponent's batting average, most wins (90), appearances, starts, complete games (102), shutouts (36), and strikeouts (1,091). In 2007, Sims became the first-ever State player to be named the ACC Player of the Year. She was first-team All-ACC three times.

Sims followed in her older sister's footsteps, picking up a softball and pitching it when she was only 5. "She has mental toughness on the mound," said Miranda Ervin, who caught her all four seasons. "She just keeps hitters off balance."

She certainly kept the hitters from Campbell off balance on May 9, 2007. That's when she tossed her fourth no-hitter of the season and the sixth one of her storied State career. Thus, Navas was used to great things from her ace and wasn't at all surprised by Sims' performance in the 1-0 win. So why all the fuss? It took the coach a minute or two to figure it out: Sims hadn't just thrown a no-hitter; she had thrown a perfect game.

Sims admitted even she didn't realize what was happening for a while. "Then I kind of figured it out in the third or fourth inning, and then in my mind, I'm like, 'Ooh, don't think about it.'" Her teammates knew it all along, talking to her but following a time-honored tradition by not mentioning the perfect game.

Nobody's perfect; we all make mistakes every day. We botch our personal relationships; at work we seek competence, not perfection. To insist upon personal or professional perfection in our lives is to establish an impossibly high standard that will eventually destroy us physically, emotionally, and mentally.

Yet that is exactly the standard God sets for us. Our love is to be perfect, never ceasing, never failing, never qualified – just the way God loves us. And Jesus didn't limit his command to only preachers and goody-two-shoes types. All of his disciples are to be perfect as they navigate their way through the world's ambiguous definition and understanding of love.

But that's impossible! Well, not necessarily if to love perfectly is to serve God wholeheartedly and to follow Jesus with single-minded devotion. Anyhow, in his perfect love for us, God makes allowance for our imperfect love and the consequences of it in the perfection of Jesus.

It's a great feeling. It's kind of an out-of-body experience.
--Abbie Sims on her perfect game

In his perfect love for us, God provides a way
for us to escape the consequences
of our imperfect love for him: Jesus.

DAY 30

DIVIDED LOYALTIES

Read Matthew 6:1-24.

"No one can serve two masters" (v. 24a).

Divided loyalties happen in the best of families; some kinfolk (admittedly from the better side of the family) cheer for the Wolfpack while some holler for the Heels or the Blue Devils. And then there's Bernie Mock.

Perhaps no one else in the state of North Carolina can match the sundered loyalties Mock encountered. He is thought to be the only basketball player in history to be a team captain for both NC State and UNC.

The upheaval produced by World War II created Mock's unique situation. He was a forward and team captain for the State "Red Terrors" in 1941 when the U.S. entered the war. As a freshman he assisted in the kidnapping of Rameses, UNC's mascot, the week of the football game. Mock joined the Marine Reserve Corps in 1942 and expected to play for State in the fall. But Uncle Sam ordered him to report to UNC for V-12 training, a program established to prepare college students for military life. "I never wanted to change schools, change teams," said Mock. "But Uncle Sam said I had to go -- so I went."

The eligibility rules were unique to the time, allowing athletes to play on teams based on where they were stationed. So Mock became the starting center for UNC. "To find myself in Chapel Hill a couple of years later, playing for the rival team, that was

strange," Mock said. His teammates went on to elect Mock their captain.

After the war, State head basketball coach Leroy Jay offered Mock a chance to play one more year, but he declined, citing the need to work to support his wife and his child.

He always had a divided loyalty. "N.C. State is my first love," he once said. "It has my heart. I'll cheer for Carolina too, sometimes -- just maybe not quite so loud."

Like Bernie Mock, you probably understand the stress that comes with divided loyalties. The Christian work ethic drives you to be successful. The world, however, often makes demands and presents images that conflict with your devotion to God: movies deride God; couples play musical beds in TV sitcoms; and TV dramas portray Christians as killers following God's orders.

It's Sunday morning and the office will be quiet or the golf course won't be crowded. What do you do when your heart and loyalties are pulled in two directions? Jesus knew of the struggle we face; that's why he spoke of not being able to serve "two masters," that we wind up serving one and despising the other. Put in terms of either serving God or despising God, the choice is stark and clear.

Your loyalty is to God -- always.

I felt sort of funny about it, playing against my former teammates.
-- Bernie Mock about the 1943-44 season

God does not condemn you for being successful
and enjoying popular culture, but your loyalty
must lie first and foremost with him.

DAY 31

PLAN AHEAD

Read Psalm 33:1-15.

"The plans of the Lord stand firm forever, the purposes of his heart through all generations" (v. 11).

Common sense and logic would dictate that the most bizarre game in the history of the ACC Tournament was the result of a grand strategy. Common sense and logic would be wrong.

In a 1968 semifinal game against sixth-ranked Duke, Norm Sloan ordered the Pack to spread the floor after the opening tip to pull Duke center Mike Lewis away from the basket. State's center, Bill Kretzer, complied by simply dribbling the ball near halfcourt, but Duke coach Vic Bubas ordered his big man not to move.

"We never intended to hold the ball," said State forward Vann Williford. "We set up to run the play the way we had planned, [and] . . . Sloan said, 'Stay right there until he comes out.' He never did." Bubas left Lewis under the basket because he felt State was too quick for his team.

Unobstructed and unharassed, Kretzer dribbled most of the half away; Duke led 4-2 at the break. In the last half, State held the ball for more than thirteen minutes after falling behind 8-6.

Another oddity of this odd game is that every time Sloan talked to a player while the clock ticked on, Duke guard Tony Barone, whom Sloan remembered as being about 5'4" tall, came over and listened in. Sloan never seemed to mind. Finally, with about three minutes left, Sloan called guard Eddie Biedenback and Williford over for a conference. Barone dutifully trotted over, too, leading Biedenback to suggest they call a time out. "If we call time-out, they'll take that midget out of the game and put in a real player," Sloan responded. He told his team to start playing.

With 2:29 left, Biedenbach nailed an 18-foot baseline jumper and then Dick Braucher scored with 40 seconds left. State won 12-10 in a game that wasn't planned that way; it just happened.

Successful living takes planning. You go to school to improve your chances for a better paying job. You use blueprints to build your home. You plan for retirement. You map out your vacation to have the best time. You even plan your children -- sometimes.

Your best-laid plans, however, sometimes get wrecked by events and circumstances beyond your control. The economy goes into the tank; a debilitating illness strikes; a hurricane hits. Life is capricious and thus no plans -- not even your best ones -- are foolproof.

But you don't have to go it alone. God has plans for your life that guarantee success as God defines it if you will make him your planning partner. God's plan for your life includes joy, love, peace, kindness, gentleness, and faithfulness, all the elements necessary for truly successful living for today and for all eternity. And God's plan will not fail.

There was no grand strategy or design. It just evolved that way after (Vic) Bubas made the decision to stay in a zone.
-- NC State forward/center Bill Kretzer

Your plans may ensure a successful life;
God's plans will ensure a successful eternity.

DAY 32

A LONG SHOT

Read Matthew 9:9-13.

"[Jesus] saw a man named Matthew sitting at the tax collector's booth. 'Follow me,' he told him, and Matthew got up and followed him" (v. 9).

We're never going to get anybody from Denver. I don't even know anybody in Denver." So spoke the head coach about a long-shot recruit.

The coach was State's Everett Case; the person he was speaking to was his assistant, Vic Bubas; the recruit about whom he was speaking was Ronnie Shavlik, who ultimately became the Atlantic Coast Conference's "first true superstar." Bubas had read in a Chicago newspaper about a 17-year-old kid who had been named the Most Promising Player in the national AAU Tournament in Denver in 1952. "He has to be awfully good to be able to accomplish this against college players and guys who were ready to go to the pros," Bubas told Case. "Maybe this kid is worth a look."

That's when Case spoke his piece about the youngster being such a long shot for State. He had a point. Shavlik grew up in Denver and expected to settle there. But coaches came calling, especially after his performance in the AAU tournament. Bubas was one of those coaches. Shavlik made some trips back East and then made his first trip ever to the South -- to Raleigh.

As he traveled, Shavlik realized he wanted to get away from Denver to "do something on my own." He liked the State campus and the people, and the Pack landed a star. Shavlik was a dominating post player, a big man with an upstoppable hook shot who could run. He still owns the State career rebounding record (1,598). The Wolfpack won the ACC all three of his varsity seasons (1954-56); he was the ACC Player of the Year in 1956 and in 1979 was inducted into the North Carolina Sports Hall of Fame.

This long shot to ever leave Denver never left North Carolina instead.

Matthew the tax collector was another long shot, an unlikely person to be a confidant of the Son of God. While we may not get all warm and fuzzy about the IRS, our government's revenue agents are nothing like Matthew and his ilk. He paid the Roman Empire for the privilege of extorting, bullying, and stealing everything he could from his own people. Tax collectors of the time were "despicable, vile, unprincipled scoundrels."

And yet, Jesus said only two words to this lowlife: "Follow me." Jesus knew that this long shot would make an excellent disciple.

It's the same with us. While we may not be quite as vile as Matthew was, none of us can stand before God with our hands clean and our hearts pure. We are all impossibly long shots to enter God's Heaven. That is, until we do what Matthew did: get up and follow Jesus.

We won't get him if we don't try.
-- Vic Bubas' response to Everett Case about recruiting Ronnie Shavlik

Only through Jesus does our status change
from being long shots to enter God's Kingdom
to being heavy favorites.

DAY 33

HERO WORSHIP

Read 1 Samuel 16:1-13.

"Do not consider his appearance or his height, for . . . the Lord does not look at the things man looks at. . . . The Lord looks at the heart" (v. 7).

David Thompson, Tommy Burleson, Monte Towe -- heroes still more than three decades after they last wore the red and white. And the player Thompson calls the "unsung hero" of the national championship team of 1974? Tim Stoddard.

Stoddard "was a guy who could do a little bit of everything -- shoot, defend, great passer," Thompson said at a 2008 gathering of the national champs. Stoddard was quite happy to be the hero in the background, the rock supporting those three All-Americas. "If David wanted me to drive him around right now, I'd be glad to drive him anywhere he wanted to go," he quipped.

Thompson pointed out that while folks still talked about the "alley oops" Towe and he connected with, Stoddard threw just as many. "It was good to have a guy like that who did the dirty work. He was kind of the enforcer," Thompson said.

Stoddard was indeed the muscle man inside. He was a 6'7", 230-pound power forward who came to Raleigh in 1971. He moved into the starting lineup as a junior that championship season and averaged 5.5 points and 4.5 rebounds per game. "My role has always been a support guy," he said. "That's fine with me."

Stoddard was also a brilliant pitcher for the Wolfpack baseball team. In three seasons, he was 16-3 with a 2.28 ERA. He pitched in the majors from 1975-88, had 26 saves one season, and pitched in two World Series. And yet, such is the legacy of that 1974 basketball team, that more than three decades later as he travels as a Christian speaker, folks still want to talk about it.

Even his kids at Northwestern, where he coaches baseball, still ask him about it. Maybe in their eyes, Stoddard is a hero. He is, after all, the only man in history who earned both World Series and NCAA basketball championship rings as an athlete.

A hero is commonly thought of as someone who performs brave and dangerous feats that save or protect someone's life. Or an athlete who excels. You figure that excludes you.

But ask your son about that when you show him how to bait a hook, or your daughter when you show up for her dance recital. Look into the eyes of those Little Leaguers you help coach.

Ask God about heroism when you're steady in your faith. For God, a hero is a person with the heart of a servant. And if a hero is a servant who acts to save other's lives, then the greatest hero of all is Jesus Christ.

God seeks heroes today, those who will proclaim the name of their hero – Jesus – proudly and boldly, no matter how others may scoff or ridicule. God knows heroes when he sees them -- by what's in their hearts.

Heroes and cowards feel exactly the same fear; heroes just act differently.
-- Boxing trainer Cus D'Amato

God's heroes are those who remain steady
in their faith while serving others.

DAY 34

THE JESUS WAY

Read Romans 13:8-14.

"The night is nearly over; the day is almost here. So let us put aside the deeds of darkness and put on the armor of light" (v. 12).

Philip Rivers did it his way, which led one ACC player to disparage him as an "ugly duckling." The thing is, the Rivers way has led him to astounding success.

Rivers is the greatest quarterback in NC State history and one of the best football has ever seen. He finished his career in Raleigh with 13,484 career passing yards, both school and ACC records and the second-highest total in NCAA history. Other school and conference records he set include career touchdown passes (95) and pass completions (1,147). His career yards-per-attempt average of 9.55 is still the best in college football history. Rivers was the ACC Athlete of the Year as a senior in 2003. He led State to four straight bowl games (winning three of them) and was the MVP in every game.

His Pro-Bowl career began when he was drafted in the first round in 2004 by the San Diego Chargers. After the 2009 season, his career passing rating was the second-best in NFL history.

All this despite the fact that -- technically speaking -- Rivers did it all wrong. While some experts decried his throwing motion, he steadfastly refused to alter what was an "unorthodox, slightly sidearm delivery" that was once compared to an "Olympic shot-putter's heave." Every time Rivers throws a ball, football purists shake their head and wonder how in the world he does it.

State offensive coordinator Marty Galbraith was firmly of the "if-it-ain't-broke-don't-fix-it" school of coaching. And Mike Canales, Rivers' position coach at State, was downright defiant, declaring, "I will never mess with his throwing motion. As someone once told me, 'He gets the ball from the hand to the man.'"

Doing it his own way, Philip Rivers has gotten the ball from his hand to the receiver as few in the history of football have done.

You have a way of life that defines and describes you. You're a die-hard NC State fan for starters. Maybe you're married with a family. A city guy or a small-town gal. You wear jeans or a suit to work every day. And then there's your faith.

For the Christian, following Jesus more than anything else defines for the world your way of life. It's basically simple in its concept even if it is downright daunting in its execution. You act toward others in a way that would not embarrass you were your day to be broadcast on Fox News. You think about others in a way that would not humiliate you should your thoughts be the plotline for a new CBS sitcom.

You make your actions and thoughts those of love: at all times, in all things, toward all people. It's the Jesus way of life, and it's the way to life forever with God.

It's almost like my trademark now.
-- Philip Rivers on his unorthodox passing style

**To live the Jesus way is to act with love
at all times, in all things, and toward all people.**

DAY 35

DRY RUN

Read John 4:1-15.

"Everyone who drinks this water will be thirsty again,
but whoever drinks the water I give him will never thirst.
Indeed, the water I give him will become in him a spring
of water welling up to eternal life" (vv. 13-14).

Seven straight times the Wolfpack had lost to UNC's basketball team -- and then came Feb. 19, 1983.

State's seven-game drought was the longest by either team in the series since the Pack teams from 1972-75 -- the David Thompson era -- had whipped the Tar Heels nine in a row. Until this night, Coach Jim Valvano had never beaten Carolina.

All the early signs indicated that the drought would continue. Carolina jumped out to a 31-24 lead and appeared on the verge of blowing the game open by halftime.

But Dean Smith, enraged over a no-call, drew a pair of technicals for protesting too vehemently. Terry Gannon made all four of the free throws, and then Lorenzo Charles was fouled and made a pair of charity shots. When Carolina turned it over, Charles hit a short jumper to give State its first lead. In just 22 seconds, a 7-point deficit had become a one-point lead.

The Wolfpack defense controlled the last half. "It's the best job defensively we have ever done," Valvano said. Still, the Tar Heels stayed close, thanks largely to State's inability to hit a free throw --only 23 of 39 for the night. Finally, in frustration during a time out, Valvano screamed, "Can anybody here make a free throw?" Cozell McQueen, only a 57.6 percent free-throw shooter, raised his hand and said, "Put me in, Coach. I can hit it."

Valvano did and he did. McQueen was fouled after an offensive rebound. Smith's time out to freeze McQueen by forcing him to think about it was a waste of time. The sophomore famously said, "My mind was a total blank." Whatever was going on up there, he hit two free throws to clinch the drought-ending 70-63 win.

You can walk across that river you boated on in the spring. The city's put all neighborhoods on water restriction, and that beautiful lawn you fertilized and seeded will turn a sickly, pale green and may lapse all the way to brown. Somebody wrote "Wash Me" on the rear window of your truck.

The sun bakes everything, including the concrete. The earth itself seems exhausted, just barely hanging on. It's a drought.

It's the way a soul looks that shuts God out.

God instilled thirst in us to warn us of our body's need for physical water. He also gave us a spiritual thirst that can be quenched only by his presence in our lives. Without God, we are like tumbleweeds, dried out and windblown, offering the illusion of life where there is only death.

Living water – water of life – is readily available in Jesus. We may drink our fill, and thus we slake our thirst and end our soul's drought – forever.

Drink before you are thirsty. Rest before you are tired.
-- Paul de Vivie, father of French cycle touring

Our soul thirsts for God's refreshing presence.

NC STATE

DAY 36

AMAZING!

Read: Luke 4:31-36.

"All the people were amazed and said to each other, 'What is this teaching? With authority and power he gives orders to evil spirits and they come out!'" (v. 36)

The most amazing individual performance in NC State football history resulted in one of the school's most amazing wins.

Senior Wolfpack halfback Dick Christy was the ACC Player of the Year and a first-team All-America in 1957. He led the Pack to a 7-1-2 record and the ACC championship. In his storied career, Christy set fourteen school records and four league records. As a sophomore, Christy averaged 7.1 yards a carry. In an amazing statistic, he averaged 45.3 yards on seven kickoff returns as a senior. He saved the best for last, though. Literally.

On Nov. 23, 1957, the ACC title hung in the balance when State met South Carolina in Columbia. The Gamecocks scored first. Christy promptly returned the kickoff 53 yards to set up his own scoring run from the three. But South Carolina took control of the game with a pair of touchdowns to lead 19-6. With less than a minute left in the half, Christy broke loose for 39 yards to the one and scored on the next play. Carolina led 19-12 at the break.

Christy scored from the one to cap State's first possession of the half. Since the Pack had missed both previous extra points, Coach Earle Edwards let Christy kick, and he tied the game. A fumble recovery set up Christy's fourth touchdown, and his kick

made it 26-19. Carolina rallied to tie the game at 26.

State mounted a late drive, but the clock ran out. USC was flagged for interference on the play, though, giving the Pack one last play after time had expired. He had never kicked a field goal, but Christy convinced Edwards to let him try a 36-yarder. The kick was good, giving State a 29-26 win and the league title.

The amazing Dick Christy had scored all 29 of State's points.

The word *amazing* defines the limits of what you believe to be plausible or usual. The Grand Canyon, the birth of your children, those last-second Wolfpack wins -- they're amazing! You've never seen anything like that before!

Some people in Galilee felt the same way when they encountered Jesus. Jesus amazed them with the authority of his teaching, and he wowed them with his power over spirit beings. People everywhere just couldn't quit talking about him.

It would have been amazing had they not been amazed. They were, after all, witnesses to the most amazing spectacle in the history of the world: God himself was right there among them walking, talking, teaching, preaching, and healing.

Their amazement should be a part of our lives because Jesus still lives. The almighty, omnipotent God of the universe seeks to spend time with us every day – because he loves us. Amazing!

It was the greatest day I've ever had on a football field.
-- Dick Christy on the South Carolina game

Everything about God is amazing,
but perhaps most amazing of all
is that he loves us and desires our company.

DAY 37

TEARS IN HEAVEN

Read Revelation 21:1-8.

"[God] will wipe every tear from their eyes. There will be no more death or mourning or crying or pain" (v. 4).

There wasn't a dry eye in the place." That described the night the Wolfpack paid tribute to their legendary coach one last time.

After a loss to Wake Forest on Dec. 5, 1964, NC State head basketball coach Everett Case called his assistants, Press Maravich and Charlie Bryant, into the shower room. In that unlikely locale, Case told the two men he was retiring and that Maravich would be the head coach with Bryant as his assistant.

Case formally announced his resignation two days later and remained with the team in an advisory capacity for the rest of the school year. His health had declined to the point that, as he put it, 'I thought I never would get home, get my clothes off and get into bed. . . . I would have liked to have finished [the season,]" Case said, "but it was not the proper thing to do."

His career over and his life soon to be, the legendary coach had one more victorious moment. The Wolfpack surprised everyone by winning the 1965 ACC Tournament. Guard and team cocaptain Tommy Mattocks recalled that as the game ended and State's players and fans exuberantly celebrated their championship, Sports Information Director Frank Weedon punched him on the shoulder and said, "Look over there, he's really enjoying this." Weedon was pointing to Case.

"On an impulse," Mattocks said, he went over and grabbed the coach and was quickly joined by other players. They hoisted him onto their shoulders and carried him onto the court where they lifted the frail man to cut the final strand of the net. It was Case, after all, who almost twenty years earlier had brought the net-cutting ceremony to North Carolina from Indiana.

"You talk about symbolism and emotion," Weedon said. "There wasn't a dry eye in the house."

When your parents died. When a friend told you she was divorcing. When you broke your collarbone. When you watch a sad movie. You cry. Crying is as much a part of life as are breathing and indigestion. Usually our tears are brought on by pain, sorrow, or disappointment.

But what about when your child was born? When State beats Duke or UNC? When you discovered Jesus Christ? Those times elicit tears too; we cry at the times of our greatest, most overwhelming joy.

Thus, while there will be tears in Heaven, they will only be tears of sheer, unmitigated, undiluted joy. The greatest joy possible, a joy beyond our imagining, must occur when we finally see Christ. If we shed tears when State wins a game, can we really believe that we will stand dry-eyed and calm in the presence of Jesus?

What we will not shed in Heaven are tears of sorrow and pain.

Are you crying? There's no crying, there's no crying in baseball.
-- Tom Hanks in A League of Their Own

Tears in Heaven will be like everything else there:
a part of the joy we will experience.

DAY 38

POWER PLAY

Read Psalm 28.

"The Lord is my strength and my shield; my heart trusts in him, and I am helped" (v. 7a).

Ben McCauley showed the whole house just how strong he was. The result was "the most dramatic, spine-tingling play" of his NC State career -- and a Wolfpack win over Wake Forest.

McCauley ended his four years in Raleigh in 2009. Three times he made the ACC All-Academic Basketball Team. The 6'9" forward-center averaged 12.4 points and 7.8 rebounds as a senior, but it was a play he made as a junior that was his most memorable moment as a member of the Wolfpack.

On Feb. 3, 2008, the 13-7 Pack hosted the 13-6 Deacons, who took a nine-point lead with 10:32 to play. But McCauley got hot, scoring eleven points down the stretch, including a three-point play that pulled the Pack to within four with about seven minutes left.

A dunk from J.J. Hickson with 2:58 left gave State its first lead of the game at 62-61. Two missed free throws gave Wake a chance to tie the game at 65 with a driving layup with only 5.2 seconds left. After a Pack timeout, Gavin Grant took the inbounds pass, hurried downcourt, and fired up a three-pointer from the right of the key with 2.7 seconds left.

"I was thinking, 'Gavin can make those shots, I've seen him make those,'" McCauley said after the game. But then he thought, "'Why not go up and see if you can get the tip-in.' No one boxed

me out. I think their whole team thought the game was over." Or headed into overtime

It wasn't. In a power play for the ages with absolutely no touch of finesse about it, McCauley stormed into the lane, rose high over teammate Javi Gonzalez, cupped the ball with his left hand, and rammed it home as the buzzer screamed. 67-65 State.

You make an honest living in a world that rewards greed and unbridled ambition. You raise your children in a world that glamorizes immoral behavior and ridicules values and parental authority. You proclaim your faith in a world that idolizes itself.

Standing tall for what you believe may get you admired, but it also makes you a target for the scoffers who fear the depth of your convictions. Living the faithful life thus requires a healthy dose of physical, mental, and emotional strength. To rely on your own strength, however, is to face the world poorly armed and woefully weak. Count on it: You will fail; the world will inevitably wear you down. Only when you admit your weakness, confess that you need some help, and allow God to be your strength will you prevail.

The strength that undergirds and supports the Christian life is not found in ourselves. Rather, it is found in the power of the Holy Spirit that lives in us.

He caught it off the rim something vicious.
      -- Wake's Harvey Hale on Ben McCauley's thundering dunk

**God did not create us ten feet tall and bulletproof,
so he lends us his own power to strengthen us
in our daily faith walk.**

DAY 39

AT A LOSS

Read Philippians 3:1-9.

"I consider everything a loss compared to the surpassing greatness of knowing Christ Jesus my Lord, for whose sake I have lost all things" (v. 8).

The Wolfpack lost Bo Rein twice.

Rein was the head football coach at State for four seasons, from 1976-79, and went 27-18-1. He faced the daunting task of following the enormously popular and successful Lou Holtz after he abruptly accepted a job to coach the New York Jets. From the first day he took the job, Rein was on the spot. He accepted the pressure with the aplomb that characterized his life. "When you get the chance for a coaching job like this one, you can't worry about who you follow or what kind of personality he had," he said.

Rein needed that confidence when his career began with three straight losses to open the 1976 season. After the Pack whipped Indiana 24-21 for Rein's first win, "everyone was jumping up and down" on the field in celebration. Such moments of triumph were rare, however, that 3-7-1 season.

Things were different after that. Rein's 1977 team went 8-4 and thumped favored Iowa State 24-14 in the Peach Bowl. The 1978 Wolfpack finished at 9-3. The regular season ended with a thrilling 24-21 win over Virginia, won on a 50-yard punt return by the head coach's younger brother, Curtis Rein. State yet again relished the underdog role in a bowl game by toppling Pittsburgh

WOLFPACK

30-17 in the Tangerine Bowl.

Rein's final team managed the unique but disappointing feat of winning the ACC title but not receiving a bowl bid though three other ACC teams did. The 1979 Pack went 7-4.

Following the season, though, as Holtz had done after four years at the helm, Rein disappointed Wolfpack fans by leaving. He accepted the head coaching job at LSU. That loss was a tough one to take, but it got harder. Less than two months later, on Jan. 10, 1980, Bo Rein, 34, died in an airplane accident.

Maybe it was when a family member died. Perhaps it wasn't so staggeringly tragic: your puppy died, your best friend moved away, or an older sibling left home. Sometime in your youth or early adult life, though, you learned that loss is a part of life.

Loss inevitably diminishes your life, but loss and the grief that accompanies it are part of the price of loving. When you first encountered loss, you learned that you were virtually helpless to prevent it or escape it.

There is life after loss, though, because you have one sure place to turn to. Jesus can share your pain and ease your suffering; but he doesn't stop there. Through the loss of his own life, he has transformed death -- the ultimate loss -- into the ultimate gain of eternal life. In Jesus lies the promise that one day loss itself will die.

It's like a death in the family.
-- Wolfpack quarterback Scott Smith on Bo Rein's death

Jesus not only eases the pain of our losses
but transforms the loss caused by death
into the gain of eternal life.

DAY 40

RESPECTFULLY YOURS

Read Mark 8:31-38.

"He then began to teach them that the Son of Man must suffer many things and be rejected by the elders, chief priests and teachers of the law, and that he must be killed" (v. 31).

They're used to losing."

I don't believe I'd-a said that, especially if I were a UConn Husky preparing to play NC State in the second round of the NCAA Tournament in 2005. But a Connecticut player did disparage the Pack, and the State players seized on the perceived lack of respect to upset the defending national champions.

"Oh, man, that was crazy," said senior Julius Hodge about the comment. "It was like no one respected the N.C. State program the way our opponents were talking about us." Hodge took the lack of respect personally and never let his teammates forget it, constantly repeating to them in the game against UConn, "Pride, respect, payback." The payback referred to the Pack's loss to Connecticut in the second-round of the 2002 NCAA Tournament.

In Worcester, Mass., 10th-seeded NC State's opening-round 75-63 win over UNC-Charlotte moved them to the second round against second-seeded UConn. With a chip on their collective shoulders, the Pack took an 11-point lead in the last half, but the Huskies rallied to tie the game at 62 with 15.8 seconds left. Hodge took the inbounds pass and hurried downcourt.

WOLFPACK

Junior forward Ilian Evtimov saw the look in Hodge's eyes and knew what was coming. "It was a look that said, 'We're not giving up, we're not letting it go, we're not losing,'" Evtimov said. Behind a pick from center Jordan Collins, Hodge drove the lane, shot, and was fouled. The basket was good, as was the free throw, and a last-second, desperate Husky heave clanked off the front rim.

The disrepected Wolfpack had earned a whole lot of respect with a 65-62 win that propelled the team into the Sweet 16.

Rodney Dangerfield made a good living as a comedian with a repertoire that was basically only countless variations on one punch line: "I don't get no respect." Dangerfield was successful because he struck a chord with his audience. No one wants to play basketball for a program that no one respects. You want the respect, the esteem, and the regard that you feel you've earned.

But more often than not, you don't get it. Still, you shouldn't feel too badly; you're in good company. In the ultimate example of disrespect, Jesus – the very Son of God -- was treated as the worst type of criminal. He was arrested, bound, scorned, ridiculed, spit upon, tortured, condemned, and executed.

God allowed his son to undergo such treatment because of his high regard and his love for you. You are respected by almighty God! Could anyone else's respect really matter?

Play for your own self-respect and the respect of your teammates.
-- Legendary Vanderbilt coach Dan McGugin

You may not get the respect you deserve,
but at least nobody's spitting on you
and driving nails into you as they did to Jesus.

DAY 41

A ROARING SUCCESS

Read Galatians 5:16-26.

"So I say, live by the Spirit. . . . The sinful nature desires what is contrary to the Spirit. . . . The acts of the sinful nature are obvious: . . . I warn you, as I did before, that those who live like this will not inherit the kingdom of God" (vv. 16, 17, 19, 21).

Their win total has long since been surpassed by other squads; others have won league championships and advanced to super regionals. But to this day, the 1968 Wolfpack baseball team remains the most successful bunch in school history.

The boys of '68 established the standard by which every other State team since the first squad in 1903 has been found wanting: They made it to the College World Series. Not only that, they were one of the last three teams standing and came within a couple of hits of winning the whole shebang.

In 1968, only the ACC champion went on, and there was no league tournament. In the season's last game, a win over Wake Forest would give State the ACC title. Second-year coach Sam Esposito gave the ball to freshman Mike Caldwell, who threw a masterpiece. He gave up a single to start the game; catcher Fred Combs gunned the runner down trying to steal. Not another Deacon reached base: 27 batters, 77 pitches. State won 4-0.

The Pack headed for the double-elimination District Three Tournament in Gastonia. Caldwell allowed only four hits in a 3-1 win over Alabama in the opener. The Pack then beat East Carolina and lost to FSU to set up a one-game showdown with the Noles. Caldwell came through yet again, and soph shortstop Darrell Moody went 4-for-5 and drove in three runs in a 4-1 win that sent the Pack to the World Series.

In Omaha, State upset Southern Illinois 7-6, lost to St. John's, beat Texas 6-5, and lost to eventual champ Southern Cal 2-0. The most successful season in NC State baseball history was over.

Are you a successful person? Your answer, of course, depends upon how you define success. Is the measure of your success based on the size of your bank balance, the square footage of your house, that title on your office door, the length of your boat?

Certainly the world determines success by wealth, fame, prestige, awards, and possessions. Our culture screams that life is all about gratifying your own needs and wants. If it feels good, do it. It's basically the Beach Boys' philosophy of life.

But all success of this type has one glaring shortcoming: You can't take it with you. Eventually, Daddy takes the T-bird away. Like life itself, all these things are fleeting. A more lasting way to approach success is through the spiritual rather than the physical. The goal becomes not money or backslaps by sycophants but eternal life spent with God. Success of that kind is forever.

We overachieved. It was amazing how many people picked us up.
-- Four-time All-ACC third baseman Chris Cammack

Success isn't permanent, and failure isn't fatal --
unless you're talking about
your relationship with God.

DAY 42

RUN FOR IT

Read John 20:1-10.

"Peter and the other disciple started for the tomb. Both were running, but the other disciple outran Peter and reached the tomb first" (vv. 3-4).

His aversion to running -- not his basketball talents -- almost kept Kenny Carr from winning an Olympic gold medal.

Frank Weedon, State's longtime sports information director, once said Carr "may have been the second greatest player to ever play here, behind David [Thompson]." Carr was quite literally behind Thompson, blossoming into the first Wolfpack star after Thompson's graduation in 1975. The duo put together a league scoring string that had never been equalled. Thompson won the ACC scoring title three times from 1973-75, and Carr won the same title in 1976 and '77, averaging 26.6 and 21.0 points per game respectively. That streak of five straight years of ACC scoring leaders from one school has never been duplicated.

Carr was a 6'8" forward and two-time All-America who UNC rival and Olympic teammate Phil Ford said was "ahead of his time." That's because Carr was "a big, strong aggressive forward who liked to step outside and take jump shots." While that type of player is common today, Carr was the exception then.

He is the only Wolfpack player to win Olympic gold (1976) and has declared the Olympics training camp experience to be "the most fun I have ever had." But he nearly didn't make it.

WOLFPACK

The 1976 team was determined to get the gold medal back where it belonged after the controversial loss in 1972 to the Russians. Coach Dean Smith held tryouts on the State campus, and Carr was one of the fifteen finalists for the twelve spots. Then he ran into trouble. Smith required that all his players run a mile under a certain time. Carr wasn't even close on his first attempt. "That was not my forte, running a mile," Carr said.

He got some assistance, though, when Indiana's Quinn Buckner helped pace Carr on his second attempt. He made it this time and ran all the way to Olympic gold.

Hit the ground running -- every day that's what you do as you leave the house and re-enter the rat race. You run errands; you run though a presentation; you give someone a run for his money; you always want to be in the running and never run-of-the-mill.

You're always running toward something, such as your goals, or away from something, such as your past. Many of us spend much of our lives foolhardily attempting to run away from God, the purposes he has for us, and the blessings he waits to give us.

No matter how hard or how far you run, though, you can never outrun yourself or God. God keeps pace with you, calling you in the short run to take care of the long run by falling to your knees and running for your life -- to Jesus -- just as Peter and the other disciple ran that first Easter morning.

On your knees, you run all the way to glory.

It was a mental thing. I just hated it.
-- Kenny Carr on running a mile in the Olympic tryouts

You can run to eternity by going to your knees.

DAY 43

BONE TIRED

Read Matthew 11:27-30.

"Come to me, all you who are weary and burdened, and I will give you rest" (v. 11).

The Red Terrors of NC State were too exhausted to play their best in the tournament semifinals. No one could blame them, however. They were using only five players.

Prior to the 1937-38 basketball season, the NCAA drastically changed the game by eliminating the jump ball after every made basket. The rule did exactly what it was expected to: It radically speeded up the game. The *Technician* sports editor didn't like the change, grumbling that "if they speed up the game any more, it will have to be played on a banked court."

State's team of 1938-39 probably would have voted for a return to the slower game of two seasons before. They became known in State lore as the "Iron Six." Coach Ray Sermon had six strong and experienced players: seniors Bill Mann, P.G. Hill, Jim Rennie, Elwin Hamilton, Sieby Jones, and junior Red Sevier. He just didn't have much else, so only rarely did anyone but the Six see action.

Then late in the season, Rennie suffered a leg injury. The Iron Five soldiered on, sometimes playing games without a substitute. Rennie hurried back, playing with a heavily bandaged leg, but then Sevier went down with an injury.

Thus, it was inevitable that the Southern Conference Tournament would simply wear the Iron Terrors down. It did but not before they displayed both stamina and heart. State beat Duke, the defending champs, 40-39 in the first round and The Citadel 40-38 in the next round. The Iron Five played all the way against The Citadel until Jones fouled out with four minutes left.

"They are the fightingest bunch of kids I ever saw," Sermon said, but they were too tired to hang with Maryland and lost in the tournament semifinals.

The everyday struggles and burdens of life beat us down. They may be enormous; they may be trivial with a cumulative effect. But they wear us out, so much so that we've even come up with a name for our exhaustion: chronic fatigue syndrome.

Doctors don't help too much. Sleeping pills can zonk us out; muscle relaxers can dull the weariness. Other than that, it's drag on as usual until we can collapse exhaustedly into bed.

Then along comes Jesus, as usual offering hope and relief for what ails us, though in a totally unexpected way. He says take my yoke. Whoa, there! Isn't a yoke a device for work? Exactly. Our mistake is in trying to do it all alone. Yoke ourselves to Jesus, and the power of almighty God is at our disposal to do the heavy lifting for us.

God's strong shoulders and broad back can handle any burdens we can give him. We just have to let them go.

They're fighting their hearts out to win, and as far as I can see they are staying in there on their nerve.
-- Coach Ray Sermon after the win over The Citadel

**Tired and weary are a way of life
only when we fail to accept Jesus' invitation
to swap our burden for his.**

DAY 44

THE SIMPLE LIFE

Read 1 John 1:5-10.

"If we confess our sins, he is faithful and just and will forgive us our sins and purify us from all unrighteousness" (v. 9).

When Tom O'Brien took over as State's head football coach in 2007, things got a lot simpler around the place.

For one thing, O'Brien doesn't like his quarterbacks to wear arm bands with the plays on them. Even the Wolfpack playbook is simpler. Once asked if his offense had more than 100 plays, O'Brien replied, "I can't remember that many. How can they?"

O'Brien's approach was no accident. He understood that the college game is not the NFL. Life for collegiate players is not just about football or hour after hour of practice and film watching. "Our coaches know about our schedules and the time conflicts and what we have to do outside football," said center Luke Lathan, who would go on to earn a postgraduate scholarship.

O'Brien kept it simple for himself also right from the first, not ending practices with a speech and not riding into the sunset in a golf cart but walking with his players to the Murphy Center.

All this was a change from the regime of Chuck Amato, whose approach to football was based on complexity. "There were a lot of plays," said tight end Marcus Stone. "Maybe it was a bit too complex for some to pick up. I thought personally we should have simplified it. The crazy thing was we'd only run 25 percent of it."

O'Brien's offensive coordinator, Dana Bible, who spent some time coaching in the NFL, said with a smile that he had never measured the Wolfpack playbook. "It's not about how many plays we have. It's about being able to execute the offense," he said.

It's about keeping it simple. And winning along the way.

Perhaps the simple life in America was doomed by the arrival of the programmable VCR. Since then, we've been on an inevitably downward spiral into ever more complicated lives. Even windshield wipers have multiple settings now, and it takes a graduate degree to figure out clothes dryers.

But we might do well in our own lives to mimic the simple formula Tom O'Brien uses. That is, we approach our lives with the awareness that success requires simplicity, a sticking to the basics: Revere God, love our families, honor our country, do our best.

Theologians may make what God did in Jesus as complicated as quantum mechanics and the infield fly rule, but God kept it simple for us: believe, trust, and obey. Believe in Jesus as the Son of God, trust that through him God makes possible our deliverance from our sins into Heaven, and obey God in the way he wants us to live. It's simple, but it's the true winning formula, the way to win for all eternity.

It's just simple. You get the simple plays right. You pound them until they don't want to fight anymore.
-- Luke Lathan on the O'Brien approach to offense

Life continues to get ever more complicated,
but God made it simple for us
when he showed up as Jesus.

DAY 45

SWEET WORDS

Read John 8:1-11.

"'Then neither do I condemn you,' Jesus declared. 'Go now and leave your life of sin'" (v. 11).

After one season, Everett Case was on the verge of leaving NC State. Then some folks showed him how much they appreciated him, and basketball history at State and in the state was changed forever.

Case's first year as State's head basketball coach was the most successful season in school history until then. The Red Terrors of 1946-47 went 26-5, won the Southern Conference Tournament, and went to the NIT, State's first-ever national postseason tournament. They finished third in the eight-team event.

Following the season, Case received an offer from a group starting a new professional team in Louisville, and it intrigued him. Moreover, the coach had "found a few things he wasn't particularly happy about at State." The Louisville group offered him a five-year contract that would have doubled his State salary. So Case made plans to fly to Louisville, along with his assistant, Carl "Butter" Anderson, and Jonas Fritch, who helped him recruit.

A simple banquet kept Case in Raleigh.

Wake Memorial Church had not yet been constructed, but was having some functions in a building. The owners of *The News & Observer* were members, and through their sports editor, they asked Case to be the featured speaker at a father and son banquet.

Since the banquet was scheduled for early in the evening to get the kids into bed on time, the coach planned to attend the banquet and then fly on to Louisville to meet with the group.

He never made it. About 10:30 p.m., Case called the sports editor and told him he was still in Raleigh. "He had changed his mind because he saw how people thought about him at the banquet." A little affirmation changed basketball history.

You make a key decision. All excited, you tell your best friend or spouse and anxiously await for a reaction. "Boy, that was dumb" is the answer you get.

A friend's life spirals out of control into disaster. Alcohol, drugs, affairs, unemployment. Do you avoid that messed-up person and pretend you don't know him?

Everybody needs affirmation in some degree. That is, we all occasionally need someone to say something positive about us, that we are worth something, and that God loves us.

The follower of Jesus does what our Lord did when he encountered someone whose life was a shambles. Rather than seeing what they were, he saw what they could become. Life is hard; it breaks us all to some degree. To be like Jesus, we see past the problems of the broken and the hurting and envision their potential, understanding that not condemning is not condoning.

After being with those kids that night, I decided Louisville was no place for me.
-- Everett Case on the banquet that kept him in Raleigh

The greatest way to affirm lost persons
is to lead them to Christ.

DAY 46

UNEXPECTEDLY

Read Matthew 24:36-51.

"No one knows about that day or hour, not even the angels in heaven, nor the Son, but only the Father" (v. 36).

While NC State's run to the 1983 national championship was a glorious surprise, equally unexpected was the 1987 ACC Tournament title.

Jim Valvano's Wolfpack got off a strong 12-4 start, but the season fell apart after that. State lost six straight games at one stretch and fell to 13-12. Valvano had a lineup that simply wasn't meshing, so he changed it. He slowed down the tempo, gave forwards Chucky Brown and Vinny Del Negro more playing time, and turned the point guard slot over to Quentin Jackson. The latter move was crucial. "Quentin settled everybody down," Del Negro said. "He brought a calmness to the team." State won its last three games.

But the Pack was only 17-15 overall, 6-8 in the ACC, and a lowly sixth seed for the tournament. "The enormity of winning the whole thing was too much," Del Negro confessed. "We approached it one game at a time, one possession at a time. That way it was manageable."

They managed the first game into a 71-64 overtime victory over 14th-ranked Duke. That game finished around midnight, so the last thing the Wolfpack needed was another one the next day. What they got was double overtime. State broke a 71-71 tie with a Brown field goal, two Del Negro free throws, and two charity shots from Bennie Bolton. State won 77-73.

The pairing in the finals looked like a bad joke. Third-ranked UNC had seven future NBA players on its roster and had whipped State easily twice during the season. But State slowed the game down, and Del Negro's free throws with 14 seconds left held up for a 68-67 upset.

NC State unexpectedly was the league champion.

Just like the folks who gave the Wolfpack no chance in 1987, we think we've got everything figured out and under control, and then something unexpected happens. About the only thing we can expect from life with any certainty is the unexpected.

God is that way too, suddenly showing up to remind us he's still around. A friend who calls and tells you he's praying for you, a hug from your child or grandchild, a lone lily that blooms in your yard -- unexpected moments when the divine comes crashing into our lives with such clarity that it takes our breath away and brings tears to our eyes.

But why shouldn't God do the unexpected? The only factor limiting what God can do in our lives is the paucity of our own faith. We should expect the unexpected from God, this same deity who caught everyone by surprise by unexpectedly coming to live among us as a man, and who will return when we least expect it.

You're never out of it in this league.
— *Quentin Jackson on the unexpected 1987 ACC championship*

**God continually does the unexpected,
like showing up as Jesus,
who will return unexpectedly.**

DAY 47

CLOCKWORK

Read Matthew 25:1-13.

"Keep watch, because you do not know the day or the hour" (v. 13).

Wolfpack guard Tommy Mattocks, who was second-team All-Tournament for the 1965 champions, had one big hole in his game: He couldn't read the Reynolds Coliseum scoreboard.

Mattocks was color blind, a malady that didn't deter him from becoming a basketball official and a baseball umpire. The problem it did create for him, however, was that when he played a home game, he could make out the scoreboard's red lights only if he looked at them from what was for him the perfect angle.

As long as a scoreboard had a dark background and was tilted somewhat, Mattocks was fine. The Reynolds scoreboard, however, sported the double whammy: It had a light background and no tilt. "Unless I got almost off the end of the court, I couldn't read it," Mattocks said.

That usually didn't create much of a problem for Mattocks, but it did serve to embarrass him pretty badly one night early in his career. As he brought the ball up the court, the scoreboard read 12 seconds to go in the first half. Mattocks, however, could see only the "two," so he reacted accordingly. From midcourt, he launched what he believed was a last-second shot.

Even as Mattocks released his bomb, head coach Everett Case "jumped up and started hollering. You could hear him over the

12,400 people in there."

It got worse. As Mattocks recalled it, "That ball 'Bammed!' off the backboard and 'Bammed!' off the rim. All the players were stunned."

They also stood around waiting for the buzzer to sound that would end the half. And they waited. And waited. "They got the rebound," Mattocks remembered. "I was standing there waiting for the buzzer to go off, but it didn't."

"I was mighty embarrassed," Mattocks said.

We may pride ourselves on our time management, but the truth is that we don't manage time; it manages us. Hurried and harried, we live by schedules that seem to have too much what and too little when. By setting the bedside alarm at night, we even let the clock determine how much down time we get. A life of leisure actually means one in which time is of no importance.

Every second of our life – all the time we have – is a gift from God, who dreamed up time in the first place. We would do well, therefore, to consider what God considers to be good time management. After all, Jesus himself warned us against mismanaging the time we have. From God's point of view, using our time wisely means being prepared at every moment for Jesus' return, which will occur -- well, only time will tell when.

Afterward it was funny, but during the game it wasn't funny at all.
— Tommy Mattocks on his scoreboard gaffe

**We mismanage our time when we fail
to prepare for Jesus' return even though
we don't know when that will be.**

DAY 48

DO WHAT YOU HAVE TO

Read 2 Samuel 12:1-15a.

"The Lord sent Nathan to David" (v. 1).

Leroy Harris did what he had to do even though he found it harder than two-a-days at NC State in the Raleigh heat. What was it that was so difficult for this easy-going giant? He had to baby-sit his son.

Harris was one of State's most versatile and best linemen. From 2003-06, he started 26 games at center, 15 at left guard, and one at right guard for the Pack. He was first-team All-ACC as a senior and did not allow a sack all season. A wrestler in high school, when he was redshirted in 2002, he wrestled for the Wolfpack and placed third in his class. Since Harris stands 6'3" and often tops the scales at 300-pounds-plus, he wrestled with the heavyweights. In 2007, he was drafted in the fourth round by the Tennessee Titans, moving into the starting lineup in 2009.

A Raleigh native, Harris was accustomed to practicing in the heat, even the rugged two-a-days of late summer. "Two-a-days are tough on your body," Harris admitted. They were particularly tough for him as he always had to sweat away some extra pounds. "But then you get to go home," he added.

That's when it really got difficult for him because waiting for him in the summer of 2006 prior to his senior season was Leroy "Tre" Harris III. Harris' wife, Christina, was working on her degree, so he helped take care of a nine-month-old boy who was

WOLFPACK

on the verge of walking. "That's definitely more tiring, mentally and physically combined," he said, laughing about his job at home. While the practices during two-a-days are soon over, "You never get to have a break from having kids. He'll wear you down."

But the devoted family man, who would team with his wife to open a drop-in day care in Nashville, just did what he had to do, both at home and on the field.

You've also had some things in your life that you did because you really had no choice. Maybe when you put your daughter on severe restriction, broke the news of a death in the family, fired a friend, or underwent surgery. You plowed ahead because you knew it was for the best or you had no choice.

Nathan surely didn't want to confront King David and tell him what a miserable reprobate he'd been, but the prophet had no choice: Obedience to God overrode all other factors. Of all that God asks of us in the living of a godly life, obedience is perhaps the most difficult. After all, our history of disobedience stretches all the way back to the Garden of Eden.

The problem is that God expects obedience not only when his wishes match our own but also when they don't. Obedience to God is a way of life, not a matter of convenience.

Coaching is making men do what they don't want, so they can become what they want to be.
-- *Legendary NFL Coach Tom Landry*

You can never foresee what God will demand of you, but obedience requires being ready to do whatever God asks.

DAY 49

PROVE IT!

Read Matthew 3.

"But John tried to deter him, saying, 'I need to be baptized by you, and do you come to me?'" (v. 14)

Every step of the way, Thurl Bailey had to prove he could play basketball.

He had to prove it to his mother. She didn't want him playing "on the dangerous playgrounds" near their home in a Washington, D.C., suburb. He went along with her decision until an AAU coach saw the 6'5" eighth grader carrying groceries home one day and talked him into giving basketball a try.

Bailey had to prove it to his junior high coach, who twice cut him from open tryouts. Bailey later said that coach "helped me more than I could ever imagine," though he told the youngster to "give up the game and quit wasting his time." Instead of quitting, Bailey found inspiration, getting to school an hour early each day to work on his game. He made the team as a junior.

Bailey had to prove it to NC State coach Norm Sloan. "Norm wasn't sold on him at all," said assistant coach Eddie Biedenbach, even though Bailey stood 6'11". All Bailey did was lead the 1983 national champions in both scoring and rebounding. He also created an iconic Wolfpack image, openly weeping with joy at midcourt after a win over North Carolina.

He had to prove it to the pros. Coach Jim Valvano had to beg the Utah Jazz to draft Bailey. He spent ten years with the team, leaving as the franchise's fifth-leading scorer.

Thurl Bailey always had something to prove. The Wolfpack faithful will always be grateful that he proved to his doubters just how good he was.

You, too, have to prove yourself over and over again in your life. To your teachers, to that guy you'd like to date, to your parents, to your bosses, to the loan officer. It's always the same question: "Am I good enough?" Practically everything we do in life is aimed at proving that we are.

And yet, when it comes down to the most crucial situation in our lives, the answer is always a decisive and resounding "No!" Are we good enough to measure up to God? To deserve our salvation? John the Baptist knew he wasn't, and he was not only Jesus' relative but God's hand-chosen prophet. If he wasn't good enough, what chance do we have?

The notion that only "good" people can be church members is a perversion of Jesus' entire ministry. Nobody is good enough – without Jesus. Everybody is good enough – with Jesus. That's not because of anything we have done for God, but because of what he has done for us. We have nothing to prove to God.

[The coach who told him to quit the game] helped me realize who I was and what I wanted.
-- Thurl Bailey on proving himself

The bad news is we can't prove to God how good we are; the good news is that because of Jesus we don't have to.

DAY 50

CELEBRATION TIME

Read Exodus 14:26-31; 15:19-21.

"Miriam the prophetess, Aaron's sister, took a tambourine in her hand, and all the women followed her, with tambourines and dancing" (v. 15:20).

Basketball fever raged on the State campus in 1929 when a conference championship touched off a spontaneous celebration.

Coach Gus Tebell was really the first head man to put State basketball on the map. In six seasons from 1925-30, he won 79 games and lost only 36. His 1928-29 squad was the fifth seed in the 16-team Southern Conference Tournament in Atlanta, but they got hot. They surprised Tennessee 48-32 behind Frank Goodwin's 23 points, got 10 points from Johnny Johnson to beat favored Clemson, and then used two Goodwin free throws in the last minute to topple heavy favorite Mississippi 34-32. The team beat Duke in the finals 44-35 with Goodwin scoring 14 and Larry Haar 13. The Red Terrors were conference champions.

Back on campus, about a hundred students "had invaded *The News & Observer* building, watching intently as the details of the [Duke] game were sent throughout the night on a direct teletype wire from Atlanta." Those exuberant students quickly spread the news about the final score. Within an hour, more than 500 students had a bonfire and a party going and were soon cruising up and down Fayetteville Street both in and atop cars.

The celebration didn't end there, starting all over again the next afternoon when the team arrived by train. This time, local citizens joined in the good times, swelling the crowd to several thousand. The players were "taken from the train steps [and] hoisted onto the shoulders of their admirers." They then clambered into cars for a short parade down Fayetteville Street to the capitol. The governor met them there, declaring, "I'd rather be captain of this championship team than to be governor."

You know what it takes to throw a good party. You start with your closest friends, add some salsa and chips, fire up the grill and throw on some burgers and dogs, and then top it all off with the NC State game on TV.

You probably also know that any old excuse will do to get people together for a celebration. All you really need is a sense that life is pretty good right now.

That's the thing about having Jesus as part of your life: He turns every day into a celebration of the good life. No matter what tragedies or setbacks life may have in store, the heart given to Jesus will find the joy in living. That's because such a life is spent with quiet confidence in God's promise of salvation through Jesus, a confidence that inevitably bubbles up into a joy the troubles of the world cannot touch. When a life is celebrated with Jesus, the party never stops.

The final buzzer set off a wild celebration on the court in Atlanta and on the campus back in Raleigh.
— Douglas Herakovich on NC State's 1929 conference title

With Jesus, life is one big party because it becomes a celebration of victory and joy.

DAY 51

REST EASY

Read Hebrews 4:1-11.

"There remains, then, a Sabbath rest for the people of God; for anyone who enters God's rest also rests from his own work, just as God did from his. Let us, therefore, make every effort to enter that rest" (vv. 9-11).

Nate Irving didn't get enough rest -- and he nearly paid for it with his life.

Irving was "arguably the Wolfpack's top defender in 2008." He missed a third of the season with a leg injury but still led the team with four interceptions, a State record for a linebacker. He led the team in tackles in five games and was honorable mention All-ACC. Irving was a pre-season All-ACC pick for the 2009 season and was poised for greatness. Starting safety Bobby Floyd said of his team-mate, "Instinctively, Nate's the best defensive player I've ever been around."

But all that promise was put on hold and nearly lost forever on June 28, 2009. Irving visited his family in Wallace and decided to make the 90-mile drive to campus rather than spending the night. He apparently fell asleep at the wheel about thirty miles from Raleigh. What resulted was "a gruesome accident that turned his sports utility vehicle into an accordion." Irving suffered cracked ribs, a separated shoulder, a collapsed lung, and a compound fracture of his left leg. When Floyd and safety Javon Walker, whose football career ended in 2009 from multiple knee injuries, visited

Irving in the hospital, they stood in silence for a while with tears in their eyes, shocked and saddened by what they saw. Irving's mother said, her son "knows he's lucky to be alive."

Irving missed the entire 2009 season, but he was cleared for spring practice in 2010. He returned a changed man. "I thought I was invincible," he said. "I've matured a lot in my decision-making," which now includes making sure he gets enough rest.

As part of the natural rhythm of life, rest is important to maintain physical health. Rest has different images, though: a good eight hours in the sack; a Saturday morning that begins in the backyard with the paper and a pot of coffee; a vacation in the mountains, where the most strenuous thing you do is change position in the hot tub.

Rest is also part of the rhythm and the health of our spiritual lives. Often we envision the faithful person as always busy, always doing something for God whether it's teaching Sunday school or showing up at church every time the doors open.

But God himself rested from work, and in blessing us with the Sabbath, he calls us into a time of rest. To rest by simply spending time in the presence of God is to receive spiritual revitalization and rejuvenation. Sleep refreshes your body and your mind; God's rest refreshes your soul.

There's nothing more important than getting your rest. I almost lost my life because I didn't get enough rest.

-- *Nate Irving*

**God promises you a spiritual rest
that renews and refreshes your soul.**

DAY 52

GOOD SPORTS

Read Titus 2:1-8.

"Show integrity, seriousness and soundness of speech that cannot be condemned, so that those who oppose you may be ashamed because they have nothing bad to say about us" (vv. 7b, 8).

In an act of sportsmanship rendered remarkable because his team had just suffered what was certainly one of the most bitter defeats of his career, Maryland head coach Lefty Driesell made his way to the State locker room to congratulate the winners and to especially heap praise on Tommy Burleson.

On March 9, 1974, top-ranked NC State and No. 4 Maryland met for what many anticipated would be the greatest championship game in the history of the ACC Tournament. No one was disappointed. The players carried on their shoulders pressure that is missing from today's league tournament. The winner advanced to the 25-team NCAA tourney with a shot at the national title; the loser went to the NIT with a shot at nothing. Six of the players in the game would be All-America; eleven of them would be drafted by the NBA.

David Thompson was his usual fantastic self, scoring 29 points, but the hero was State's 7'4" senior center. Burleson had what was called "the greatest individual performance in the greatest game ever played in ACC history." He poured in 38 points and grabbed 13 rebounds. But Maryland hit a phenomenal 61 percent of its shots, and regulation play ended in a 97-97 tie. Monte Towe's free throws with six seconds left in OT clinched the 103-100 win.

Driesell sought the tourney MVP out after the game. "That's the greatest game I've ever seen a big man play," he told Burleson. "That's one heck on an effort, Tommy." His good sportsmanship continued when he urged the Pack to "go on now and win the whole thing," -- which, of course, they did.

One of life's paradoxes is that many who would never consider cheating on the tennis court or the racquetball court to gain an advantage think nothing of doing so in other areas of their life. In other words, the good sportsmanship they practice on the golf course or even on the Monopoly board doesn't carry over.

They play with the truth, cut corners, abuse others verbally, run roughshod over the weak and the helpless, and generally cheat whenever they can to gain an advantage on the job or in their personal relationships.

But good sportsmanship is a way of living, not just of playing. Shouldn't you accept defeat without complaint (You don't have to like it.); win gracefully without gloating; treat your competition with fairness, courtesy, generosity, and respect? That's the way one team treats another in the name of sportsmanship. That's the way one person treats another in the name of Jesus.

One person practicing sportsmanship is better than fifty preaching it.
-- Knute Rockne

Sportsmanship -- treating others with courtesy, fairness, and respect -- is a way of living, not just a way of playing.

DAY 53

HOMELESS

Read Matthew 8:18-22.

"Jesus replied, 'Foxes have holes and birds of the air have nests, but the Son of Man has no place to lay his head'" (v. 20).

For most of the season, one of the most successful teams in State baseball history had no home field on which to play; in effect, the Pack was homeless.

The 2003 team went 45-18, finished third in the ACC, played host to a regional for the first time in school history, and also advanced to a Super Regional for the first time ever. Coach Elliott Avent was named the National, the Atlantic Region, and the ACC Coach of the Year.

With such success, the team should have been playing before thousands of cheering fans in Doak Field. Instead, the squad played thirty road games before it ever played at home, and the regional State hosted was played at Fleming Stadium in Wilson.

State's home ballpark was undergoing $4.2 million worth of renovations, forcing the team to hit the road. State's first game at Doak Field -- on April 2 against UNC-Greensboro (a 3-2 win) -- marked the seventh site where the Wolfpack had hosted a game. They played in Kinston, Buies Creek, Zebulon, and Wilson, the field at Clayton High School, and the Durham Bulls home park.

Practice was an even bigger problem than finding game sites. The team often used the basement of Reynolds Coliseum, which

at least had batting cages and a pitching mound, and frequently hopped on a bus to various high school fields for practice.

Despite being homeless, the team won. State was 23-7 and ranked No. 12 in the nation when it finally played at home. Even then, though, the Pack didn't play before thousands of ardent supporters. The renovations weren't complete, so seating was limited to the first 800 fans who showed up. They sat in the grandstand section along third base. At least admission was free.

Rock bottom in America has a face: the bag lady pushing a shopping cart; the scruffy guy with a beard and a backpack at the interstate exit holding a cardboard sign. Look closer at that bag lady or that scruffy guy, though, and you may see desperate women with children fleeing violence, veterans haunted by their combat experiences, or sick or injured workers.

Few of us are indifferent to the homeless when we're around them. They often raise quite strong passions, whether we regard them as a ministry or a nuisance. They trouble us, perhaps because we realize that we're only one catastrophic illness and a few paychecks away from joining them. They remind us, therefore, of how tenuous our hold upon material success really is.

But they also stir our compassion because we serve a Lord who – like them -- had no home, and for whom, the homeless, too, are his children.

Personally, I love road trips.
   -- Wolfpack pitcher Vern Sterry on the 2003 team's travels

**Because they, too, are God's children,
the homeless merit our compassion, not our scorn.**

DAY 54

CHEAP TRICKS

Read Acts 19:11-20.

"The evil spirit answered them, 'Jesus I know, and I know about Paul, but who are you?'" (v. 15)

Man, how big is your playbook?" That question came right across the line of scrimmage, but that perplexed defender hadn't seen anything yet; the trick plays were still to come.

On Jan. 1, 2003, 10-3 NC State took on 10-2 Notre Dame in the Gator Bowl. Because the opposition was the Irish, the game gave the Pack some valuable national exposure. Chuck Amato and his team thus pulled out all the stops that included a set of bewildering trick plays. The plays were so complex and so numerous that a frustrated Notre Dame defender asked the question about the size of the Wolfpack playbook early in the game. His inquiry was directed across the line to senior tight end Sean Berton, who couldn't help but laugh. "I told him it's not a playbook," Berton said. "It's playbooks."

Especially did the offense for the Gator Bowl make use of a variety of trick plays. For instance, wideout Bryan Peterson, a former high school quarterback, threw three passes, completing two for 27 yards. His pass to tight end Joe Gray came after he caught a cross-field lateral from Pack quarterback Philip Rivers, the intended target of the one pass Peterson missed.

State also threw the "Rooster" play at the bewildered Irish. On the play, Rivers lined up about two steps behind center Jed

WOLFPACK

Paulsen with tailback T.A. McLendon in front of him to his right. Rivers took the snap from Paulsen, tucked the ball between McLendon's legs, carried out a fake and ran right as McLendon went to the left. The play worked for a 3-yard TD run.

With the trick plays and the regular old plays working, State routed the overmatched Irish 28-6 to complete the first 11-win season in school history.

Scam artists are everywhere — and they love trick plays. An e-mail encourages you to send money to some foreign country to get rich. That guy at your front door offers to resurface your driveway at a ridiculously low price. A TV ad promises a pill to help you lose weight without diet or exercise.

You've been around; you check things out before deciding. The same approach is necessary with spiritual matters, too, because false religions and bogus Christian denominations abound. The key is what any group does with Jesus. Is he the son of God, the ruler of the universe, and the only way to salvation? If not, then what the group espouses is something other than the true Word of God.

The good news about Jesus does indeed sound too good to be true. But the only catch is that there is no catch. No trick -- just the truth.

When you run trick plays and they work, you're a genius. But when they don't work, folks question your sanity.
-- Bobby Bowden

God's promises through Jesus sound too good to be true, but the only catch is that there is no catch.

DAY 55

IDENTITY CRISIS

Read Matthew 16:13-20.

"[Jesus] asked his disciples, 'Who do people say the Son of Man is?' They replied, 'Some say John the Baptist; others say Elijah; and still others, Jeremiah or one of the prophets'" (vv. 13-14).

Roman Gabriel's identity in football history is clear: He was a quarterback. At State, though, he got his biggest kick out of playing defense.

Gabriel chose State over 71 other scholarship offers because he wanted to stay close to his hometown of Wilmington and the Pack coaches had no problem with his playing football, basketball, and baseball. Gabriel was a player before his time, the "prototype for today's strong-armed, oversized quarterbacks who look more like tight ends or linebackers than signal callers."

In fact, Gabriel did see some action at linebacker for State. He played in an age (1958-61) when ten players had to play both offense and defense with one sub allowed. Not surprisingly, most teams alternated their quarterback. But Gabriel liked playing defense, and he was so good at it that defensive coordinator Al Michaels wanted him on the field, though Coach Earle Edwards was never particularly excited about the idea. Sometimes at practice when Edwards' attention was elsewhere, Gabriel would sneak into the defensive drills.

As a sophomore in 1959, Gabriel saw action at cornerback and safety and moved up to linebacker in goal-line situations. In 1960, with State clinging to a 3-0 lead over North Carolina and the Heels at the one, linebacker Gabriel nailed the quarterback on a sneak, causing a fumble that Claude "Hoot" Gibson snared and ran out to the 29. State won 3-0.

Despite his defensive prowess, Gabriel was first and foremost a quarterback. He was All-America and twice the ACC Player of the Year. He set or shared 22 Wolfpack records.

You may not be Spider Man or the Caped Crusader or a linebacker disguised as a quarterback, but you do have a secret identity, don't you? It's hidden by the face you put on to meet the world each day, the expression that masks your longing to sail around the world or write a novel or how much you hate your job.

You are, in fact, more than what you appear. The world does not know your depth, but you shouldn't feel too badly about the shortsightedness of others. Many people still can't figure out who Jesus is.

But that's not because Jesus failed to declare who he was; he told folks repeatedly. In like manner, what matters is not what others do not know about you but what they know for sure: That you are a Christian. That, above all else, should be your identity.

Deep inside, we're still the boys of autumn, that magic time of the year that once swept us on to America's fields.
                                                            -- Archie Manning

Many folks still don't know Jesus
for who he is, but everyone should recognize you
as one of his followers.

CHANGING TIMES

Read Romans 6:1-14.

"Just as Christ was raised from the dead through the glory of the Father, we too may live a new life" (v. 4).

When young women started crawling through the windows of the men's bathroom to get into a basketball game, the times were changing at NC State.

Everett Case's success "turned the area's admiration for the Red Terrors into a flaming infatuation." That change in devotion and fanaticism had immediate consequences, dooming Thompson Gym and bringing about the construction of Reynolds Coliseum.

Prior to the UNC game of Feb. 25, 1947, the Raleigh fire chief sent word that -- in accordance with state fire regulations -- unless every fan had a seat, he would cancel the game. Every seat was filled ninety minutes prior to the tip-off, and arena personnel locked the doors, forcing reporters to crawl through a window after showing proper ID.

Fans also found various ways to get in. They ripped one gym door off its hinges and also scrambled through windows. Freshman Red Terror Norm Sloan and teammate Dick Dickey were in the men's rest room next to the team's locker room standing at the urinal when the window above them shattered and a girl crawled through. "She didn't slow down at all," Sloan recalled, "She just came right on it, ran right by us and went upstairs to the court."

Officials announced that if folks without seats didn't leave, the game would be cancelled. They responded by "crunching into the bleachers and doubling up" or hiding in the basement, leaving room for more folks to pour into the aisles. Thirty minutes before tip-off, the fire chief cancelled the game; he then had to be escorted to safety by local police as the sullen crowd didn't appreciate his devotion to their safety and berated him with rocks and curses.

Basketball times had changed in Raleigh.

Anyone who asserts no change is needed in his or her life isn't paying attention. Every life has doubt, worry, fear, failure, frustration, unfulfilled dreams, and unsuccessful relationships in some combination. The memory and consequences of our past often haunt and trouble us.

Recognizing the need for change in our lives, though, doesn't mean the changes that will bring about hope, joy, peace, and fulfillment will occur. We need some power greater than ourselves or we wouldn't be where we are.

So where can we turn to? Where lies the hope for a changed life? It lies in an encounter with he who is the Lord of all Hope: Jesus Christ. For a life turned over to Jesus, change is inevitable. With Jesus in charge, the old self with its painful and destructive ways of thinking, feeling, loving, and living is transformed.

A changed life is always only a talk with Jesus away.

The crowd that night informed the state legislature that times were changing on the Raleigh campus.
* -- Writer Douglas Herakovich on the impact of the UNC non-game*

In Jesus lie the hope and the power
that change lives.

DAY 57

THE NIGHTMARE

Read Mark 5-1-20.

""What do you want with me, Jesus, Son of the Most High God? Swear to God that you won't torture me!" (v. 7)

The starting tailback was late for the bus and was benched. The team blew a 28-point lead and would lose if the opposing team's kicker hit a 39-yard field goal. It was a nightmare!

On Sept. 21, 2002, the 17th-ranked, 4-0 Wolfpack took on Texas Tech in Lubbock. The day didn't start out too well when freshman tailback T.A. McLendon failed to show up at the team bus on time. He was benched instead of making his first career start.

That didn't seem to matter, however, because once McLendon got onto the field, he ran all over Tech's defense for 150 yards and tied a school record with five rushing touchdowns. Meanwhile, junior quarterback Philip Rivers, who had a surprise pre-game visit from legendary basketball coach Bobby Knight, was chunking the ball all over the Texas plains for 301 yards.

All that offense meant that the Pack chewed up yardage and put up points by the bunch. With seven minutes left in the third quarter, State led 38-10. "Hey, I thought it was over," said defensive end Shawn Price, who returned a fumbled snap 35 yards for a touchdown. The Texas boys with their prolific offense surely didn't think the game was over. Throw a whole lot of passes, draw some key penalties, nab an interception -- and what you've got is a Texas-sized nightmare.

Tech tied the game at 45 and then lined up with 39 seconds left to kick what would probably be a game-winning field goal. That's when State woke up from the nightmare. The kick was wide left, and the game went into overtime. After a Tech field goal, McLendon scored from the 8-yard line. State won 51-48 and went to 5-0 for the first time since 1991.

Falling. Drowning. Standing naked in a crowded room. Blowing a 28-point lead. They're nightmares, dreams that jolt us from our sleep in anxiety or downright terror. The film industry has used our common nightmares to create horror movies that allow us to experience our fears vicariously. This includes the formulaic "evil vs. good" movies in which demons and the like render good virtually helpless in the face of their power and ruthlessness.

The spiritual truth, though, is that it is evil that has come face to face with its worst nightmare: Jesus. We seem to understand that our basic mission as Jesus' followers is to further his kingdom and change the world through emulating him in the way we live and love others. But do we appreciate that in truly living for Jesus, we are daily tormenting the very devil himself?

Satan and his lackeys quake helplessly in fear before the power of almighty God that is in us through Jesus.

I can't have a nightmare tonight. I've just lived through one.
-- Darrell Imhoff, the opposing center the night Wilt Chamberlain scored
100 points.

As the followers of Jesus Christ,
we are the stuff of Satan's nightmares.

NC STATE

DAY 58

TO TELL THE TRUTH

Read Matthew 5:33-37.

*"Simply let your 'Yes' be 'Yes,' and your 'No,' 'No';
anything beyond this comes from the evil one" (v. 37).*

The truth was too awful to believe, but Lou Pucillo had to face up to it: The nuns had lied to him.

When Pucillo was an eighth grader, the nuns at his school in Philadelphia told his class that if they promised to go to church for nine straight days and then fulfilled that promise, their dreams would come true. Pucillo complied, and he had only one dream: He wanted to play basketball at a major university. But Pucillo didn't make the school team as a freshman or a sophomore and didn't even try out his junior year, convinced he would just get cut again. He made the team his senior year but played sparingly.

Pucillo had never grown into his dreams. At his graduation in 1955, he was only 5'9" tall and weighed only 157 pounds. Facing up to the dreadful truth that the nuns had lied to him, Pucillo enrolled in Temple Prep School to take a few college-prep courses. Temple had a basketball team, and Pucillo tried out and made it. Flashing his passing skills and deadly jump shot for the first time, he averaged more than 25 points a game for a 25-1 team.

State assistant coach Vic Bubas saw Pucillo play and liked what he saw. Two huge problems remained: Head coach Everett Case liked big point guards, which Pucillo clearly wasn't, and he liked point guards that were always in control. Pucillo was "as tightly reined as a tornado. He was an unabashed hot dog" whose flashy game reflected his gregarious personality.

Both Bubas and Pucillo won over The Old Gray Fox. In 1959, Pucillo, the smallest player Case ever signed to a scholarship at NC State, was the ACC Player of the Year and the ACC Athlete of the Year. He was a first-team All-America and was inducted into the North Carolina Sports Hall of Fame in 1991.

It turned out those nuns had told the truth after all.

No, that dress doesn't make you look fat. But, officer, I wasn't speeding. I didn't get the project finished because I've been at the hospital every night with my ailing grandmother. What good-looking guy? I didn't notice.

Sometimes we lie to spare the feelings of others; more often, though, we lie to bail ourselves out of a jam, to make ourselves look better to others, or to gain the upper hand over someone.

But Jesus admonishes us to tell the truth. Frequently in our faith life we fret about what is right and what is wrong, but we can have no such ambivalence when it comes to telling the truth or lying. God and his son are so closely associated with the truth that lying is ultimately attributed to the devil ("the evil one"). Given his character, God cannot lie; given his character, the devil lies as a way of life. Given your character, which is it?

Trampling on the truth has become as commonplace as overpaid athletes and bad television.
                                              -- Hockey coach Dan Bauer

Jesus declared himself to be the truth,
so whose side are we on when we lie?

DAY 59

ANSWERING THE CALL

Read 1 Samuel 3:1-18.

"The Lord came and stood there, calling as at the other times, 'Samuel! Samuel!' Then Samuel said, 'Speak, for your servant is listening'" (v. 10).

Jim Ritcher absolutely, positively did not want to play on the offensive line for NC State. But the team needed him to step across the line, so he answered the call and became the greatest offensive lineman in school history.

As a senior center in 1979, Ritcher won the Outland Trophy as the nation's best lineman. He was a two-time All-America. In 1987, his jersey number was retired, and in 1998, he was inducted into the College Football Hall of Fame.

Ritcher wasn't even considering NC State in high school until he attended a banquet where coach Lou Holtz and twins Dave and Don Buckey (See Devotion No. 6.) were present. "I really liked them and fell in love with the way they walked about State," Ritcher recalled. One visit to the campus sealed the deal.

But "things were not instantly lovely for him" in Raleigh. First of all, that coach he had liked so much took off for the bright lights of New York and the Jets. But there was more.

"It was sort of funny," Ritcher recalled about a time that wasn't laughable at all when it happened. One of the first things new head coach Bo Rein did upon taking over was contact his recruits. he told Ritcher, "We still want you for the same position. By the way, what position is that?" Though he had played both defensive end and offensive tackle in high school, Ritcher's response was both clear and absolute: He wanted to play defense.

At Ritcher's first day of practice as a Wolfpack, though, Rein asked him to switch to center. "I complained and did everything but leave" was Ritcher's response. He insisted he would not be able to learn the new position. Rein wasn't moved, the head coach telling his rookie player it would all work out for the best.

"It did," Ritcher said, "but I would never have believed it."

A team player is someone who does whatever the coach calls upon him to do for the good of the team. Something quite similar occurs when God places a specific call upon a Christian's life.

This is much scarier, though, than shifting positions on a football team as Jim Ritcher did. The way many folks understand it is that answering God's call means going into the ministry, packing the family up, and moving halfway around the world to some place where folks have never heard of air conditioning, fried chicken, paved roads, or the Wolfpack. Zambia. The Philippines. Cleveland even.

Not for you, no thank you. And who can blame you?

But God usually calls folks to serve him where they are. In fact, God put you where you are right now, and he has a purpose in placing you there. Wherever you are, you are called to serve him.

I actually started to like the center position. It didn't seem too bad.
-- Jim Ritcher on his freshman season on the offensive line

God calls you to serve him right now
right where you are.

DAY 60

DREAM WORLD

Read Joshua 3.

"All Israel passed by until the whole nation had completed the crossing on dry ground" (v. 17b).

Kay Yow had long cherished a dream that had nothing to do with the scoreboard or a whole season of wins. One night in 2007, her dream came true.

Feb. 16, 2007, turned out to be one of the most spectacular nights in the history of NC State's women's basketball. It was Senior Night, which is always fun. More than that, however, before the start of the game, the university's board of trustees had voted to name the Reynolds Coliseum court after Yow. This was, therefore, the first-ever game played on Kay Yow Court.

That the opponent on this night was second-ranked North Carolina (25-1) added another measure of excitement. That the State women were no slouches at 18-8 overall and 7-4 in the conference ensured that fans would pack the house to see an old-fashioned barnburner.

They got it. Early on, the Wolfpack blew UNC out of the gym, rushing to a 26-point lead with three minutes left in the half. UNC finally woke up, though, and began chipping away at the mammoth lead. When 6-foot-7 center Gillian Goring fouled out with a full seven minutes to play and State suddenly couldn't find the basket with a flashlight, Carolina began a charge. The Heels cut the lead to three points with 1:36 left. But Ashley Key nailed a basket to make it 68-63, and UNC got no closer. Key nailed four free throws down the stretch and State won 72-65.

Beating Carolina always makes for a memory. But it's what happened at the buzzer that made Yow's dream come true. In their excitement, exuberance, and joy, the student body rushed onto the floor. Yow had seen that happen on TV for other teams and had wished it for hers. On that night, her dream came true.

No matter how tightly or doggedly we cling to our dreams, devotion to them won't make them a reality. Moreover, the cold truth is that all too often dreams don't come true even when we put forth a mighty effort. The realization of dreams generally results from a head-on collision of persistence, timing, and luck.

But what if our dreams don't come true because they're not the same dreams God has for us? That is, they're not good enough and in many cases, they're not big enough.

God calls us to great achievements because God's dreams for us are greater than our dreams for ourselves. Could the Israelites, wallowing in the misery of slavery, even dream of a land of their own? Could they imagine actually going to such a place?

The fulfillment of such great dreams occurs only when our dreams and God's will for our lives are the same. Our dreams should be worthy of our best – and worthy of God's involvement in making them come true.

It brought tears to my eyes and I'm not an emotional person.
-- Kay Yow on the students' charging the floor after the UNC win

**If our dreams are to come true, they must be
worthy of God's involvement in them.**

DAY 61

IMPORTANT STUFF

Read Matthew 6:25-34.

"Seek first his kingdom and his righteousness, and all these things will be given to you as well" (v. 33).

Everett case was so dedicated to basketball that he made sure he was buried in a spot that allowed him to keep in touch with the Wolfpack, even in death.

The legendary NC State coach (See Devotion No. 32.) had one priority in his daily life: basketball. While he encouraged his players to take advantage of the scholarship they received by getting their degrees, he let them know what should be on their minds once March rolled around. For instance, Smedes York came to practice late one day during the week of the ACC Tournament. He walked in "about an hour late, with his slide rule still in his pocket." York was a civil engineering student, and he had what seemed like a good excuse for his tardiness: He had been in a lab. That didn't sit well with Case, though. "This is tournament week, boy," he told York. "Forget all that crap!"

Even after declining health forced him to retire two games into the 1964-65 season, Case couldn't leave basketball. He took a trip down to Gainesville, Fla., to visit former player Norm Sloan, the Gators' head man. Sloan was preparing his team for North Carolina, and while he was there, Case showed up every day at practice. Finally, the day before the game, he shouted to Sloan, "In the ACC we can't give out scouting information on other schools, but they can't play against a zone."

Case died on April 30, 1966, in his apartment. His will let everyone know that basketball would be his priority even in the next world. Case requested that he be buried on a hill overlooking Highway 70, which was then the main drag out of Raleigh. From there, he could wave to his team as it rode off to play North Carolina, Duke, and Wake Forest.

Basketball may not be the most important thing in your life, but you do have priorities. What is it that you would surrender only with your dying breath? Your family? Every dime you have? Your NC State season tickets?

What about God? Would you denounce your faith in Jesus Christ rather than lose your children? Or everything you own?

God doesn't force us to make such unspeakable choices; nevertheless, followers of Jesus Christ often become confused about their priorities because so much in our lives clamors for attention and time. It all seems so worthwhile.

But Jesus' instructions are unequivocal: Seek God first. Turn to him first for help, fill your thoughts with what he wants for you and your life, use God's character as revealed in Jesus as the pattern for everything you do, and serve and obey him in all matters, at all moments.

God – and God alone – is No. 1.

If you've ever heard me at a press conference, the first thing I do is give honor to God because he's first in my life.
-- College basketball coach Gary Waters

God should always be number one in our lives.

DAY 62

IN A WORD

Read Matthew 12:33-37.

"For out of the overflow of the heart the mouth speaks. The good man brings good things out of the good stored up in him, and the evil man brings evil things out of the evil stored up in him" (vv. 34b-35).

The situation was so bleak that coach Norm Sloan didn't know what to say to his team. So he just muttered a few bromides and sent them back onto the court -- where they proceeded to pull an impossible comeback against the greatest dynasty in college basketball history.

State and UCLA, winner of seven straight national titles, met in the semifinals of the 1974 NCAA Tournament. The confrontation was an epic, tied 35-35 at the half, 65-65 at the end of regulation, and 67-67 after the first OT. When the Bruins opened the second overtime with seven straight points, "it appeared that the old king was once again ready to reclaim his throne."

For some reason, though, UCLA called a time out with 2:07 left, which, if nothing else, broke the Bruins' momentum. It certainly didn't give the Wolfpack coach occasion for some momentous, inspiring words. "They had the ball out of bounds, and I didn't know what to say to my team," Sloan recalled, "I just told them . . . somebody better make something good happen quickly."

Practically everybody turned out to be that somebody. Monte Towe drew a charge and made both free throws. David Thompson then got a steal and a basket. After a UCLA free throw made it 75-71, Tommy Burleson scored. UCLA tried to stall the game away, but Tim Stoddard intercepted a pass; Burleson was fouled and hit a free throw with 1:38 left. 75-74.

After UCLA missed a free throw, Thompson's driving basket propelled the Pack into the lead. Two Thompson free throws with 34 seconds left gave State a 78-75 cushion. They won 80-77.

Even if their coach had been pretty much at a loss for words.

These days, everybody's got something to say and likely as not a place to say it. Talk radio, 24-hour sports and news TV channels, late-night talk shows. Talk has really become cheap.

But words still have power, and that includes not just those of the talking heads, hucksters, and pundits on television, but ours also. Our words are perhaps the most powerful force we possess for good or for bad. The words we speak today can belittle, wound, humiliate, and destroy. They can also inspire, heal, protect, and create. Our words both shape and define us. They also reveal to the world the depth of our faith.

We should never make the mistake of underestimating the power of the spoken word. After all, speaking the Word was the only means Jesus had to get his message across – and look what he managed to do.

We must always watch what we say, because others sure will.

It wasn't any brainstorm on my part.
– Norm Sloan on what he said to his team in the 2:07 time out

Choose your words carefully; they are the most powerful force you have for good or for bad.

MEMORY LOSS

Read 1 Corinthians 11:17-29.

"[D]o this in remembrance of me" (v. 24).

The White Shoes Gang, the first bowl win, the first home night game, a win over a national power -- the 1967 Wolfpack football season was one to remember.

Earle Edwards' team went 8-2 in the regular season, the best record since the 1927 squad of Gus Tebell went 9-1 and won the Southern Conference championship. The key to the season was the defense, dubbed the White Shoes Gang by senior linebacker Chuck Amato.

The Pack was 3-0 when it flew to Houston to meet the 2nd-ranked Cougars. The Gang set up two touchdowns, both by tailback Bobby Hall. Houston trailed 10-6 with time running out when All-American Fred Combs intercepted a pass and returned it 39 yards. State won 16-6, a victory once described as "the most monumental in the school's history."

History was made on Oct. 21 when Wake Forest came to town for the first-ever night game at Carter Stadium. Combs had a 71-yard punt return for a touchdown, quarterback Jim Donnan, the ACC Player of the Year, hit All-ACC wide receiver Harvey Martell for a TD, the backs ran for more than 300 yards, and the Gang shut Wake down the last half. The result was a 24-7 win.

The Wolfpack took on Georgia in the Liberty Bowl where the White Shoes Gang stole the show. Donnan to Martell made it

7-0, and halfback Tony Barchuk scored from the one for a 14-7 State lead in the fourth quarter. Twice the Gang turned Georgia away in the closing minutes. Defensive back Bill Morrow made a fourth-down stop at the one; then after a blocked State punt, the Gang forced Georgia into four incomplete passes from the nine. The 14-7 win was State's first-ever in a bowl.

All in all, 1967 was a season for Pack fans to remember.

Memory makes us who we are. Whether our memories are dreams or nightmares, they shape us and to a large extent determine both our actions and our reactions. Alzheimer's is so terrifying because it steals our memory from us, and in the process we lose ourselves. We disappear.

The greatest tragedy of our lives is that God remembers. In response to that memory, he condemns us for our sin. On the other hand, the greatest joy of our lives is that God remembers. In response to that memory, he came as Jesus to wash even the memory of our sins away.

Through memory, we encounter revival. At the Last Supper, Jesus instructed his disciples and us to remember. In sharing this unique meal with fellow believers and remembering Jesus and his actions, we meet Christ again not just as a memory but as an actual living presence. To remember is to keep our faith alive.

Men forget everything; women remember everything. That's why men need instant replay in sports. They've already forgotten what happened.
-- Comedienne Rita Rudner

We remember Jesus,
and God will not remember our sins.

DAY 64

YOU NEVER KNOW

Read Exodus 3:1-12.

"But Moses said to God, 'Who am I, that I should go to Pharaoh and bring the Israelites out of Egypt?' And God said, 'I will be with you'" (vv. 11-12a).

On the night of Jan. 12, 1983, any hopes the Wolfpack had for a season to remember came to an end. Ah, but you never know.

Against Virginia that night, guard Dereck Whittenburg broke his foot. The loss was devastating for the team. Whittenburg "was the irreplaceable leader, the guy who would take a game-winning shot without blinking, someone who would say, 'Let's go, boys,' and know that there would be a dozen guys behind him."

By morning, pundits were writing the Wolfpack off. Coach Jim Valvano faced up to what was being said, telling his team, A lot of people . . . are saying our season is over." But, he continued, "Something good is going to happen to us."

Valvano made major adjustments to the team's style of play and tempo. He turned to a half-court motion game that could use freshman Ernie Myers' driving ability.

Early on, predictions of doom looked to be on the mark when the team lost five of its next seven games and fell to 9-7. But things were happening nonetheless. Terry Gannon scored more. Lorenzo Charles and Cozell McQueen took on added responsibilities inside and grew up quickly. Thurl Bailey took over the post scoring, and forwards Harold Thompson and Alvin Battle stepped up their games. Point guard Sidney Lowe became the leader on the court.

What resulted was a team with a more well-rounded attack instead of one that relied on shooting guards and fast breaks. And when Whittenburg did return -- well, they were ready.

The night the season apparently ended turned out to be the night that led directly to a national title. You just never know.

You never know what you can do until -- like the '83 Wolfpack -- you want to bad enough or until – like Moses -- you have to. Serving in the military, maybe even in combat. Standing by a friend while everyone else unjustly excoriates her. Undergoing agonizing medical treatment and managing to smile. You never know what life will demand of you.

It's that way too in your relationship with God. As Moses discovered, you never know where or when God will call you or what God will ask of you. You do know that God expects you to be faithful and willing to trust him even when he calls you to tasks that daunt and dismay you.

You can respond faithfully to whatever God calls you to do for him. That's because even though you never know what lies ahead, you do know that God will both lead you and provide what you need.

There's one word to describe baseball: You never know.
— *Yogi Berra*

You never know what God will ask you to do,
but you always know he will provide
everything you need to do it.

THE CONQUERORS

Read John 16:19-33.

"In this world you will have trouble. But take heart! I have overcome the world" (v. 33b).

No father. Gangs threatening to kill him. Kicked out of school. No one to take him in. And he overcame it all to become one of NC State's greatest basketball players.

Anthony Grundy finished his Wolfpack career by leading the Pack to the second round of the 2002. NCAA Tournament. He led the team for three seasons in both scoring and steals; he was first-team All-ACC in 2002. As a senior in 2002, the 6'3" guard was the first State player ever to lead the team in scoring, rebounding, assists, and steals.

The truth is that the college game wasn't nearly as difficult for Grundy as what he had to overcome just to get to Raleigh. He grew up in Louisville with no father. In high school, a street gang promised to kill him. To protect himself, he brought a gun to school, was caught, and was kicked out of school. The kid who was supposed to kill him was himself murdered within a year.

High-school coach Kris Vance stepped in. He called Tim Colovos, a youth pastor in Bowling Green, Kent., who was 27, single, and white, and asked him to take in a black teenager with a history. He did. Because state high-school officials believed Grundy's move resulted from recruitment, he needed a court injunction just to play basketball his senior year.

Grundy accepted a scholarship from Bradley University, but when he made his ACT scores he wanted more options. When Bradley refused to release him, he appealed to the NCAA on the grounds that Pastor Colovos, who had signed the letter of intent, was not his legal guardian. The NCAA sided with Grundy, and the rest is Wolfpack basketball history.

We often hear inspiring stories of people who triumph by overcoming especially daunting obstacles as Anthony Grundy did. Those barriers may be physical or mental disabilities or great personal tragedies or injustice. When we hear of them, we may well respond with a little prayer of thanksgiving that life has been kinder to us.

But all people of faith, no matter how drastic the obstacles they face, must ultimately overcome the same opponent: the Satan-infested world. Some do have it tougher than others, but we all must fight daily to remain confident and optimistic.

To survive from day to day is to give up by surrendering our trust in God's involvement in our daily life. To overcome, however, is to stand up to the world and fight its temptations that would erode the armor of our faith in Jesus Christ.

Today is a day to overcome by remaining faithful. The very hosts of Heaven wait to hail the conquering hero.

It's a blessing from God that Anthony has persevered through so much. I always felt he had a guardian angel watching over him.
                                        -- Former high school coach Kris Vance

**Life's difficulties provide us a chance
to experience the true joy of victory in Jesus.**

DAY 66

YOUNG BLOOD

Read: Jeremiah 1:4-10.

*"The Lord said to me, 'Do not say, 'I am only a child' . . .
for I am with you and will rescue you'" (vv. 7a, 8).*

R.J. Mattes was about to do something few people his age ever did, and he was nervous about it.

The evening of Sept. 3, 2009, Mattes needed to talk to his dad, so he texted him. He was a lot like his dad, especially when it came to size. R.J. was always a head taller than his classmates growing up. In the sixth grade, he outgrew a pair of jeans and gave them to a neighbor to wear. The neighbor was 30 years old at the time. As R.J. grew up, he shared an interest with his dad: football.

R.J.'s father was Ron Mattes, who played defensive lineman for Virginia and went on to a seven-year pro career as an offensive lineman. Tom O'Brien coached the Cavalier offensive linemen at the time, and he frequently traded barbs with the trash-talking Mattes, barking at him to get back across the line of scrimmage where he belonged. Mattes' response was always to tell O'Brien to get somebody who could block him.

Shortly after O'Brien was hired as the head coach at State, Ron Mattes gave his old practice nemesis some film of his son and said R.J. was better than he had been at that age. That was good enough for O'Brien, who offered a scholarship that R.J. accepted.

And so there he was, so nervous he needed some affirmation from his dad. Why? Because the next day, redshirt freshman R.J.

WOLFPACK

Mattes was starting at right offensive guard for the Wolfpack against South Carolina. He was the youngest lineman to start for State since Leroy Harris in 2003 and one of only four freshmen starting on the line in the entire ACC.

His dad told his son he was ready. "You know your plays. You know everything. Get all the nerves out and go out there and play," his dad said. R.J. did. He started the first eight games of the 2009 season before an injury sidelined him.

While the media seem inordinately obsessed with youth, most aspects of our society value experience and some hard-won battle scars. Life usually requires us to spend time on the bench as a reserve, waiting for our chance to play with the big boys and girls. You probably rode some pine in high school. You started college as a lowly freshman. You began work at an entry-level position. Even head football coaches learn their trade as assistants.

Paying your dues is traditional, but that should never stop you from doing something bold right away, as R.J. Mattes did. Nowhere is this truer than in your faith life. You may well assert that you are too young and too inexperienced to really do anything for God. Those are just excuses, however, and God won't pay a lick of attention to them when he issues a call.

After all, the younger you are, the more time you have to serve.

You're only young once, but you can be immature forever.
-- Former major leaguer Larry Andersen

Youth is no excuse for not serving God;
it just gives you more time.

DAY 67

OLD-FASHIONED WAY

Read Leviticus 18:1-5.

"You must obey my laws and be careful to follow my decrees. I am the Lord your God" (v. 4).

Undefeated NC State was trailing North Carolina 17-7 in the third quarter. The Pack had the greatest passing quarterback in school history to load up and pull off a comeback. Instead, State went out and played some old-fashioned football.

State was 6-0 and ranked 14th in the nation on Oct. 12, 2002, when 2-3 Carolina came to town and took a 10-7 halftime lead. Senior tackle Scott Kooistra made a halftime plea to offensive coordinator Marty Galbraith, but head coach Chuck Amato was the one who decided to do exactly what Kooistra had asked for.

After UNC made it 17-7 early in the third quarter, the time had apparently arrived to turn State's all-time passing leader, Philip Rivers, and his fast receivers loose. Instead, Amato spoke quite decisively into his headset to his coaches in the box high overhead: "If you throw the dadgum football, I'm going to come up there and get after you."

State went to old-fashioned, smashed-mouth football, which Kooistra had said they should do. They ran and ran and ran some more and simply blew Carolina off the line of scrimmage in the process. While tailbacks T.A. McLendon and Josh Brown did their part, the heroes were the hawgs up front: Kooistra, tackle Chris Colmer, guards Sean Locklear and Shane Riggs, center Jed Paulsen, and tight ends Joe Gray and Sean Berton. An excited Kooistra described the carnage: "Once we got to running in the second half, it was like blood in the water. We were the sharks."

UNC was helpless before the old-fashioned onslaught. When the last play had been run, State had run to a 34-17 win.

To speak of a football team as "old-fashioned" is to describe a laudable style of play. Usually, though, to refer to some person, some idea, or some institution as old-fashioned is to deliver a full-fledged insult. They're out of step with the times and the mores, hopelessly out of date, totally irrelevant, and quite useless.

For the people of God, however, "old-fashioned" is exactly the lifestyle we should pursue. The throwbacks are the ones who value honor, dignity, sacrifice, and steadfastness, who can be counted on to tell the truth and to do what they say. Old-fashioned folks shape their lives according to eternal values and truths, the ones handed down by almighty God.

These ancient laws and decrees are still relevant to contemporary life because they direct us to a lifestyle of holiness and righteousness that serves us well every single day. Such a way of living allows us to escape the ultimately hopeless life to which so many have doomed themselves in the name of being modern.

It was a beauty to see. Here we have a Heisman Trophy candidate in Philip Rivers and he's handing the ball off.
                                        -- Chuck Amato on the win over UNC

**The ancient lifestyle God calls us to still leads us
to a life of contentment, peace and joy,
which never grows old-fashioned.**

DAY 68

GOOD LUCK

Read 1 Samuel 28:3-20.

"Saul then said to his attendants, 'Find me a woman who is a medium, so I may go and inquire of her'" (v. 7).

At one stretch in his career at NC State, Everett Case's Wolfpack beat North Carolina fifteen straight times. As it turned out, the wins really had nothing to do with talent or coaching. It was the brown suit.

In the early 1940s, UNC was the state's top dog. Case changed that immediately. He whipped the Heels the first time he played them, 48-46 on Feb. 1, 1947, and went on to beat them fourteen more times before he finally lost.

A lot of talent dribbled through Raleigh and contributed to the great streak. Center Paul Horvath started all four years (1948-51), helping the Pack to 111 wins. Dick Dickey (1947-50), the first player in the area to use a jump shot consistently, set a school record with 1,644 points and made All-America teams three times. Sammy Ranzino (1948-51) promptly broke Dickey's record, setting a mark that would stand until David Thompson came along.

After win no. 14 in the streak on Jan. 26, 1952, Case explained that the Wolfpack had something extra that accounted for all the wins over UNC: his Carolina suit. "I've worn it at every Carolina game," he told a reporter. "That's the truth. It stays in mothballs between Carolina games now."

On one occasion, though, the suit was seriously endangered.

WOLFPACK

Dorothy Fritch, a longtime friend, once went through the bachelor's closet to help with spring cleaning. She laid out a big pile of clothes to be taken away; the Carolina suit was in the pile. When Case spotted it, he exclaimed, "My Lord, Dorothy! You can't give that away! That would be like losing (center) Bobby Speight."

The suit stayed.

Black cats are right pretty. A medium is a steak. A key chain with a rabbit's foot wasn't too lucky for the rabbit. And what in the world is a blarney stone? About as superstitious as you get is to say "God bless you" when somebody sneezes.

You look indulgently upon good-luck charms (such as brown suits), tarot cards, astrology, palm readers, and the like; they're really just amusing and harmless. So what's the problem? Nothing as long as you conduct yourself with the belief that superstitious objects and rituals – from broken mirrors to your daily horoscope – can't bring about good or bad luck. You aren't willing to let such notions and nonsense rule your life.

The danger of superstition lies in its ability to lure you into trusting it, thus allowing it some degree of influence over your life. In that case, it subverts God's rightful place.

Whether or not it's superstition, something does rule your life. It should be God – and God alone.

I'm no more superstitious than any other basketball coach. I just don't like to take chances.

-- Everett Case on the Carolina suit

**Superstitions may not rule your life, but
something does; it should be God and God alone.**

DAY 69

DECISIONS, DECISIONS

Read John 6:60-69.

"The words I have spoken to you are spirit and they are life. Yet there are some of you who do not believe" (vv. 63b-64a).

Norm Sloan made three decisions affecting NC State and his coaching career, one he regretted and two he did not.

Sloan was recruited by Everett Case out of the Navy in 1946. He was a key part of squads that posted a 55-8 record and won the 1947 and '48 Southern Conference championships. In 1949, though, Sloan abruptly left the team in midseason. "After plenty of soul searching," he decided to join the football team in its spring drills to prepare for the 1949 season.

"I loved basketball, and everything was going so well for the program," Sloan said. So why in the world would he make such a radical decision? He was thinking after life after graduation: "I wanted to go into coaching, and I found out that if you wanted to coach basketball, you had to coach football too. That's just the way it was at that time."

That decision apparently worked out quite well as Sloan was never without a coaching job after he graduated in 1951. He was the head coach at Florida with an 85-63 record when State came calling in 1966 and he had another decision to make. He decided to return home. "I would not have left Florida for any institution in the nation except North Carolina State University," he said.

That decision worked out quite well also, resulting in the most successful period in State basketball history. But then Sloan made a decision that he always regretted. After 266 wins and a national title in fourteen seasons, he decided to return to Florida.

Sloan's feelings about that decision ultimately were different from the others he had made. "I wish I hadn't done it," he later said. "It turned out that N.C. State was home for us."

As with Norm Sloan, the decisions you have made along the way have shaped your life at every pivotal moment. Some decisions you made suddenly and carelessly; some you made carefully and deliberately; some were forced upon you. You may have discovered that some of those spur-of-the-moment decisions have turned out better than your carefully considered ones.

Of all your life's decisions, however, none is more important than one you cannot ignore: What have you done with Jesus? Even in his time, people chose to follow Jesus or to reject him, and nothing has changed; the decision must still be made and nobody can make it for you. Ignoring Jesus won't work either; that is, in fact, a decision, and neither he nor the consequences of your decision will go away.

Carefully considered or spontaneous – how you arrive at a decision for Jesus doesn't matter; all that matters is that you get there.

They were our people, our school. It's just where we belonged.
-- Norm Sloan on why he regretted his decision to leave State

A decision for Jesus may be spontaneous or considered; what counts is that you make it.

DAY 70

A CHANGE OF PLANS

Read Genesis 18:20-33.

"The Lord said, 'If I find fifty righteous people in the city of Sodom, I will spare the whole place for their sake'" (v. 26).

The Wolfpack coaches and players had everything all planned out for the 2010 conference baseball tournament: play, get lots of sleep, play. They had to change their plans, though; that sleep part just didn't work out.

Little was expected of State in the tournament since the Pack was the No. 7 seed and had three teams ranked in the top 20 in the way. But State came out hot, whipping No. 16 Clemson 13-8 on Wednesday afternoon.

That left the Pack with plenty of time to rest and prepare for No. 6 Georgia Tech on Friday night. The game started right on time at 8 p.m., but after that, all of the Pack's carefully laid plans were laid to rest. Rain started falling in the first inning. After almost two hours, the umps gave up and rescheduled the game for 10 a.m. Saturday. Tech pounded the Pack 17-5.

State had no time to dwell on the rout and little time to go about its planned down time because the next game was at 8 that night. The Pack surprised No. 18 Virginia Tech 10-9. Nobody planned for the game to go into extra innings, but it did, not concluding until 1:23 a.m.

The win propelled State into the championship game -- at 1

p.m. Sunday. "I don't think the timing of the night will have any effect on us," said sophomore catcher Pratt Maynard about the unplanned, short turnaround time after a 15-hour day. State hung tough against a well rested FSU team, leading 3-2 in the seventh inning before falling 8-3.

They had plenty of time to plan for lots of sleep before their next game, though. The strong showing in the ACC Tournament helped land the 38-22 Wolfpack in the NCAA Tournament.

To be unable to adapt to changing circumstances to is stultify and die. It's true of animal life, of business and industry, of the military, of sports teams, of you and your relationships, your job, and your finances. Changing your plans regularly therefore is rather routine for you.

But consider how remarkable it is that the God of the universe may change his mind about something. What could bring that about? Prayer. Someone -- an old nomad named Abraham or a 21st-century Wolfpack fan like you -- talks to God, who listens and considers what is asked of him.

You may feel uncomfortable praying. Maybe you're reluctant and embarrassed; perhaps you feel you're not very good at it. But nobody majors in prayer at school, and as for being reluctant, what have you got to lose? Your answer may even be a change of plans on God's part. Such is the power of prayer.

You can do two things with your head down: play golf and pray.
-- Lee Trevino

Prayer is powerful;
it may even change God's mind.

DAY 71

COMEBACK KIDS

Read Acts 9:1-22.

"All those who heard him were astonished and asked, 'Isn't he the man who raised havoc in Jerusalem among those who call on this name?'" (v. 21)

No odds seem to be too big to overcome." So spoke a confident Philip Rivers. But 24-0 in a bowl game? Nope, not even that.

On Dec. 28, 2000, the 7-4 Wolfpack took on the 6-5 Minnesota Golden Gophers in the Micronpc.com Bowl in Miami. The real NC State players must have missed the bus to the stadium and arrived late because early in the second quarter Minnesota led 24-0. You would think panic would have set in, but since the Pack had made a habit of pulling off comebacks all season, they stayed cool and collected though they were in real trouble. "It's amazing how calm we were in the huddle," Rivers said. "We have this air about us that we'll come around and get it done."

They did, pulling off what was called their "most incredible, improbable comeback yet" in rallying past Minnesota 38-30.

It started when Rivers, the game's MVP with 24 of 39 passes for 310 yards and two touchdowns, hit tight end Andy Vanderveer with a 2-yard TD toss that completed a 72-yard drive. "That was a little spark," Rivers said. State trailed 24-8 at halftime.

The spark became a flame in the third quarter, ignited by a blocked punt by safety Brian Williams. Koren Robinson, who set a bowl record with 157 receiving yards, scored on a reverse on the next play. 24-16. Kent Passingham booted a 37-yard field goal. 24-19. Koren Robinson caught a 58-yard bomb to the 3, and Ray Robinson barreled in from there. Incredibly, the Wolfpack led 25-24.

In the fourth quarter, the Pack led 31-30 when defensive tackle Ricky Fowler stripped the ball and linebacker Corey Lyons recovered at the Gopher 8. Robinson got the call and scored from there. Senior linebacker Clayton White picked off a Gopher Hail Mary pass with 1:12 to go to complete the incredible comeback.

Life will have its setbacks whether they result from personal failures or from forces and people beyond your control. Being a Christian and a faithful follower of Jesus Christ doesn't insulate you from getting into trouble. Maybe severe financial problems suffocated you. A serious illness sidelined you. Or your family was hit with a great tragedy. Life is a series of victories and defeats. Winning isn't about avoiding defeat; it's about getting back up to compete again. It's about making a comeback of your own.

When you avail yourself of God's grace and God's power, your comeback is always greater than your setback. You are never too far behind, and it's never too late in life's game for Jesus to lead you to victory, to turn trouble into triumph. As it was with the Wolfpack against Minnesota and with Paul, it's not how you start that counts; it's how you finish.

We were down 24-0, and 24-0 to some teams means it's over. But not to this team.

-- Philip Rivers

In life, victory is truly a matter of how you finish and whether you finish with Jesus at your side.

DAY 72

PAYBACK

Read Matthew 5:38-42.

"I tell you, Do not resist an evil person. If someone strikes you on the right cheek, turn to him the other also" (v. 39).

The Wolfpack got their revenge; in the process they also got the ACC Tournament championship.

The Virginia Cavaliers of the early 1980s featured Ralph Sampson, the only player other than UCLA's Bill Walton to win three straight national Player of the Year Awards. Not many people beat Virginia in those days, and that included NC State. The Pack had lost seven straight to the Cavaliers.

State's three seniors in 1982-83 -- Sidney Lowe, Thurl Bailey, and Dereck Whittenburg -- weren't intimidated by Sampson as they had played with him at high-school all-star games. As a result, the Pack played Virginia close. In Jim Valvano's first two seasons, his team had lost by an average of only 6.7 points. But they still lost.

None of the losses stuck in the collective Wolfpack craw more than that of Feb. 26, 1983. It was Whittenburg's first game back after missing fourteen contests with a broken foot. Cavalier fans taunted State in the closing minutes of the 86-75 game by chanting "N-I-T! N-I-T! N-I-T." "That was ugly," Lowe commented about the insult. "And God don't like ugly."

Thus, the Wolfpack were eager to tackle the Cavs in the tournament finals, but they couldn't contain Sampson inside in the first half. Reserve guard Terry Gannon's outside shooting kept the

Wolfpack close as they trailed only 40-37 at the break.

In the last half, though, Bailey fronted Sampson, and Lorenzo Charles, Cozell McQueen, and Alvin Battle alternated pushing him around under the basket. State went on a late run to grab a 75-66 advantage with 4:20 to play before Virginia fought back. Whittenburg's two late free throws clinched the 81-78 win that sealed the championship -- and the payback.

The very nature of an intense rivalry is that the loser will seek payback for the defeat of the season before. But what about in life when somebody's done you wrong; is it time to get even?

The problem with revenge in real-life is that it isn't as clear-cut as a scoreboard. Life is so messy that any attempt at revenge is often inadequate or, worse, backfires and injures you.

As a result, you remain gripped by resentment and anger, which hurts you and no one else. You poison your own happiness while that other person goes blithely about her business. The only way someone who has hurt you can keep hurting you is if you're a willing participant.

But it doesn't have to be that way. Jesus ushered in a new way of living when he taught that we are not to seek revenge for personal wrongs and injuries. Let it go and go on with your life. What a relief!

Man, I'd like to pay them back for that in a big way.
    -- Walt Densmore to his teammates during the "N-I-T" chant

**Resentment and anger over a wrong injures you,
not the other person, so forget it --
just as Jesus taught.**

DAY 73

NAME DROPPING

Read Exodus 3:13-20.

"God said to Moses, 'I AM WHO I AM. This is what you are to say to the Israelites: 'I AM has sent me to you'" (v. 14).

Like the animal's name it bears, the NC State nickname for its athletic teams was once endangered.

In the early days of athletics at North Carolina A&M, the teams were tagged the "Farmers." During the 1922 football season, a State fan wrote a letter to athletic officials, declaring that "as long as State's players behaved on and off the field like a wolfpack," the team wouldn't win. The student newspaper published the letter, which amused and bemused the student body. Students began referring to the football team as the Wolfpack; the name stuck.

The basketball team remained the "Farmers" until the 1924 season when coach Richard Crozier dressed his team in brilliant red uniforms. The students picked up on the red and dubbed the squad the "Red Terrors."

In 1946, Chancellor J.W. Harrelson announced that he detested the football team's nickname. "The only thing lower than a wolf is a snake in the grass," he said. He reminded the school's many World War II veterans that "wolfpack" had been the name given to Nazi submarines. He came up with a contest to choose a new nickname, offering season football tickets as prizes.

Among the suggestions he received were the North Staters, the

WOLFPACK

Cotton Pickers (with a plow mule for a mascot), the Cardinals (the state bird), the Cultivators, the Pine Rooters (the name given to pigs in some Carolina counties), and the Auctioneers. The huge favorite, however, was the Wolfpack.

Harrelson's efforts failed. A year later all of NC State's athletic teams became known as the Wolfpack.

Nicknames are not slapped haphazardly upon teams or upon individuals. In the case of people, they usually reflect widely held perceptions about the person named. Proper names do that also.

Nowhere throughout history has this concept been more prevalent than in the Bible, where a name is not a mere label but is an expression of the essential nature of the named one. That is, a person's name reveals his or her character. Even God shares this concept; to know the name of God is to know God as he has chosen to reveal himself to us.

What does your name say about you? Honest, trustworthy, a seeker of the truth and a person of God? Or does the mention of your name cause your coworkers to whisper snide remarks, your neighbors to roll their eyes, or your friends to start making allowances for you?

Most importantly, what does your name say about you to God? He, too, knows you by name.

The wolf is a scrappy, tough animal -- the spittin' image of our team.
-- Anonymous 1946 writer supporting the Wolfpack mascot

**Live so that your name evokes
positive associations by people you know,
by the public, and by God.**

DAY 74

REVELATION

Read Isaiah 53.

"But he was pierced for our transgressions, he was crushed for our iniquities; the punishment that brought us peace was upon him, and by his wounds we are healed" (v. 5).

From coaching to advertising to various radio and TV deals to motivational speaking and on to athletics administration, Jim Valvano was many things simultaneously. As he proved in a 1985 halftime tirade, he was also a bit of a prophet.

For point guard Nate McMillan, "playing for NC State was a far-fetched goal." Clemson was the only ACC school to recruit him out of high school, but he didn't even have the grades to get into a major college. He wound up at Chowan Junior College in Murfreesboro where Valvano found him as part of the celebrated recruiting class of 1984 that included Chris Washburn, Quentin Jackson, John Thompson, and Vinny Del Negro. McMillan was an immediate "leader on a team that lacked discipline." He helped the Wolfpack to the Final Eight in both 1985 and '86.

Still, playing pro ball wasn't even a dream McMillan had. Until the night of Feb. 9, 1985. No one except McMillan had played very well in the first half against SMU, and at halftime Valvano let his players know how he felt about it. As he dressed his team down, the coach issued his startling prediction: "If everybody made the same effort and played the way Nate McMillan comes to play, we could be winning this game. That guy there will play 10 years in the NBA."

That surprised McMillan, but Valvano was right on. The guy who was never a star in high school, college, or in the NBA had a 12-year career in the pros. His jersey was retired by the Seattle Supersonics and Chowan College and honored by NC State.

In our jaded age, we have relegated prophecy to dark rooms where mysterious women peer into crystal balls or clasp our sweaty palms while uttering vague generalities. At best, we understand a prophet as someone who predicts future events as Jim Valvano did that night in the State locker room.

When we open the pages of the Bible, though, we encounter something radically different. A prophet is a messenger from God, one who relays divine revelation to others.

Prophets seem somewhat foreign to us because in one very real sense the age of prophecy is over. In the name of Jesus, we have access to God through our prayers and through scripture. In searching for God's will for our lives, we seek divine revelation. We may speak only for ourselves and not for the greater body of Christ, but we do not need a prophet to discern what God would have us do. We need faith in the one whose birth, life, and death fulfilled more than 300 Bible prophecies.

I gave up a long time ago trying to predict the future and trying to deal with things I couldn't deal with.
                                                                      -- Brett Favre

**Persons of faith continuously seek a word
from God for their lives.**

DAY 75

WITNESS PROTECTION

Read Hebrews 11:39-12:2.

"Therefore, since we are surrounded by such a great cloud of witnesses, . . . let us run with perseverance the race marked out for us" (v. 12:1).

Overflow crowds and a generous action from the student body contributed to the completion of Memorial Bell Tower.

NC State's most notable symbol was constructed as a monument to the alumni killed in World War I. Thirty-three alums died in the war, but the memorial plaque contains 34 names as G.L. Jeffers, Class of '13, was erroneously reported as killed in action. When the mistake was discovered, the decision was made to alter the extra name. It was changed to G.E. Jefferson to symbolize the unknown soldiers from State and elsewhere.

The Great Depression caused fundraising efforts for the tower to lag, and then World War II further delayed the tower's completion. After the war, money was still needed to finish the construction. Some of that money resulted from a creative idea that took advantage of a real problem.

Veterans returning home after World War II swelled enrollment at State to almost 5,000. Each student had the chance to purchase season basketball tickets, and they bought all 3,200 passes to Thompson Gym. This meant that only students could attend the games: no faculty, no alumni, no students' wives or dates.

WOLFPACK

During the 1946-47 season, the student government proposed students give up their passes to the Davidson game so the tickets could be sold to the general public. In a referendum, 93 percent of the students voted for the idea. More than 2,500 tickets were sold at $1.50 each with all the money going toward the tower.

More than likely, you don't have an overflow crowd jamming your home or office to applaud your efforts every day as the Wolfpack do in the gym. You don't have TV cameras broadcasting your every move to an enthralled audience. Sometimes you may even feel alone. A child's illness, the slow death of a loved one, financial troubles, worries about your health – you feel isolated.

But a person of faith is never alone, and not just because you're aware of God's presence. You are always surrounded by a crowd of God's most faithful witnesses, those in the present and those from the past. Their faithfulness both encourages and inspires. They, too, have faced the difficult circumstances with which you contend, and they remained faithful and true to God.

With their examples before you, you can endure your trials, looking in hope and faithfulness beyond your immediate troubles to God's glorious future. Your final victory in Christ will be even sweeter because of your struggles.

In sports and acting, you're in front of a crowd, and you like to hear the fans cheer.
– Actress Dana Hill

The person of faith is surrounded by a crowd of witnesses whose faithfulness in difficult times inspires us to remain true to God no matter what.

DAY 76

PARTY TIME

Read Luke 15:1-10.

"There is rejoicing in the presence of the angels of God over one sinner who repents" (v. 10).

The players bounded up walls and directed the band; the fans started chanting. They were just celebrating, that's all.

On Nov. 10, 2007, the Wolfpack outlasted the Tar Heels 31-27 at Carter-Finley. "Just another day at the ballpark," joked State head coach Tom O'Brien after the wild and unpredictable game that went right down to the final seconds. State trailed 27-24 late in the game when defensive end Willie Young hit the Heel quarterback as he tried to pass, and the ball fell right into the arms of defensive tackle DeMario Pressley at the UNC 28.

O'Brien turned the offense over to sophomore tailback Jamelle Eugene. Despite a sprained left ankle, Eugene carried six straight times. He finally scored from the one for the last of his career-high 159 yards rushing on 32 carries. The score and the conversion gave State a 31-27 lead with only 1:41 to play.

But it wasn't over. The Heels converted a fourth-and-ten and hit an 18-yard pass to hurry downfield to the Wolfpack 7 as the clock rolled under a minute. Three incompletions set up an all-or-nothing play: fourth down with 6.9 seconds left. In the huddle, senior Pack cornerback Jimmie Sutton III was ready. "You have to block things out and know you have to make a play," he said.

He did. The Heels went his way, lofting a fade pass into the end zone. Sutton won the battle, grabbing the ball to end the game and set off a celebration that was as wild as the contest itself. Wide receivers Darrell Blackman and Darrell Davis bounded up a wall to high-five some students. Delirious fans chanted "Tom O'Brien, Tom O'Brien!" Eugene led his own celebration, turning into a conductor and directing the State band in the fight song.

It was party time down South! Time to celebrate!

State just whipped Carolina. You got that new job or that promotion. You just held your newborn child in your arms. Life has those grand moments that call for celebration. You may jump up and down and scream in a wild frenzy or share a quiet, sedate candlelight dinner at home -- but you celebrate.

Consider then a celebration that is beyond our imagining, one that fills every niche and corner of the very home of God and the angels. Imagine a celebration in Heaven, which also has its grand moments.

Celebrations of such magnitude are touched off when someone comes to faith in Jesus. Heaven itself rings with the joyous sounds of the singing and dancing of the celebrating angels. Even God rejoices when just one person – you or someone you have introduced to Christ -- turns to him.

When you said "yes" to Christ, you made the angels dance.

There's so much joy and excitement.
-- State tight end Marcus Stone after the 2007 win over UNC

God himself joins the angels
in heavenly celebration when even a single person
turns to him through faith in Jesus.

DAY 77

FATHERS AND SONS

Read Luke 3:1-22.

"And a voice came from heaven: 'You are my Son, whom I love; with you I am well pleased'" (v. 22).

Before there was the Pistol, there was Press.

When Peter Press Maravich was born in 1947, his father, Press, announced the birth at halftime of a semipro basketball game. As Pete grew up around the high-school teams Press coached, "if you saw Press, you saw Pete." An assistant coach said, Pete "always wanted to be around Press, but Press was always around basketball." As it was with Everett Case, the man he succeeded as head coach at State, Press Maravich didn't just love basketball; it was an obsession for him.

When he was the head coach at Clemson, Press showed off his son by having the 9-year-old dribble on concrete with gloves on and then blindfolded. Press came up with about forty drills and exercises for his son. They called them Homework Basketball. Together, they "worked at the edge of art and science" to produce what they called "Showtime." In the process, the father and son team created a legend who played the game like no else before.

For a while, it seemed that the legend would play for NC State. Maravich was Case's hand-picked successor as head coach when he retired in 1964. The Pack went 21-5 and won the ACC Tournament in Maravich's first season at the helm. His son, meanwhile, was averaging 32.5 points a game at a Raleigh high school. They planned for Pete to play for Press at NC State.

But the son couldn't make the SAT scores required to matriculate at State. On April 30, 1966, after only two seasons and a 39-14 record, Press bolted for LSU, taking the Pistol with him.

Contemporary American society largely belittles and marginalizes fathers and their influence upon their sons. Men are perceived as necessary to effect pregnancy; after that, they can leave and everybody's better off.

But we need look in only two places to appreciate the enormity of that misconception: our jails – packed with males who lacked the influence of fathers in their lives as they grew up -- and the Bible. God – being God – could have chosen any relationship he desired between Jesus and himself, including society's approach of irrelevancy. Instead, the most important relationship in all of history was that of father-son.

God obviously believes that a close, loving relationship between fathers and sons, such as that of Press and Pete Maravich, is crucial. For men and women to espouse otherwise or for men to walk blithely and carelessly out of their children's lives constitutes disobedience to the divine will.

Simply put, God loves fathers. After all, he is one.

My dad was a huge influence on me. I imagine if he had put a wrench in my hand I would have been a great mechanic.
                                                                -- Pete Maravich

Fatherhood is a tough job, but a model
for the father-child relationship is found
in that of Jesus the Son with God the Father.

DAY 78

I CAN'T STAND IT!

Read Exodus 32:1-20.

"[Moses'] anger burned and he threw the tablets out of his hands, breaking them to pieces at the foot of the mountain" (v. 19).

Vinny Del Negro was one frustrated basketball player, but State fans remain grateful he didn't handle it the way his father did.

Del Negro never doubted he could be a star. Jim Valvano apparently didn't believe it, though. For two and a half years, Del Negro mostly sat on the bench watching Spud Webb, Terry Gannon and Nate McMillan man the guard spots for the Wolfpack. "There is no question that frustration set in," Del Negro said.

His support came from his dad: "My father told me, 'Vinny, if you are good enough, the coach will play you.'" The senior Del Negro knew about frustration with a coach and how not to handle it. Del Negro the elder was a two-time junior college All-America in the 1950s who played briefly for Adolph Rupp at Kentucky. When Rupp bumped him from the starting lineup a few games into the season, Vin Del Negro responded to the frustration of being benched by quitting.

His son may have had the same urge. In fact, six of his would-be teammates transferred during Del Negro's first two seasons. But he stayed and worked hard to become so good Valvano would have to play him. That's exactly what happened.

The frustration ended in January 1987, Del Negro's junior season, when he moved into the starting lineup against Georgia Tech. In the ACC tournament, he hit the winning free throws with 14 seconds left to beat North Carolina and won the Everett Case Trophy as the tourney's MVP. He was first-team All-ACC as a senior in 1987-88 and eventually was named one of the top 25 players in San Antonio Spurs history.

It was all worth the wait.

The traffic light catches you when you're running late for work or your doctor's appointment. The bureaucrat gives you red tape when you want assistance. Your daughter refuses to take her homework seriously. Makes your blood boil, doesn't it?

Frustration is part of God's testing ground that is life even if much of what frustrates us today results from man-made organizations, bureaucracies, and machines. What's important is not that you encounter frustration—that's a given—but how you handle it. Do you respond with curses, screams, and violence? Or with a deep breath, a silent prayer, and calm persistence, and patience?

It may be difficult to imagine Jesus stuck in traffic or waiting for hours in a long line in a government office. It is not difficult, however, to imagine how he would act in such situations, and, thus, to know exactly how you should respond. No matter how frustrated you are.

I let frustration creep in at times, but I knew if I just continued to work and watch that my opportunity to play would come.
-- Vinny Del Negro

Frustration is a vexing part of life,
but God expects us to handle it gracefully.

DAY 79

CLOTHES HORSE

Read Genesis 37:1-11.

"Israel loved Joseph more than all his children, because he was the son of his old age: and he made him a coat of many colours" (v. 3 KJV).

The shoes. That's how Tommy DiNardo knew he was a Wolfpack basketball player.

Growing up, DiNardo dreamed of playing basketball for NC State, just as his father, Phil, had. The senior DiNardo was a forward for Everett Case's ACC champions in 1954, '55, and '56. He was team captain as a junior and a senior.

When no major schools recruited the younger DiNardo out of high school, he accepted a scholarship to Louisburg Junior College. His roommate was Quinton Leonard, who had shunned small-school offers to pursue his dream of playing ball for State.

The fast friends transferred to State in the fall of 1981. Leonard walked on and earned the team's only available position despite going through the try-outs with an extremely painful dislocated shoulder. He played 17 minutes in eight games during the 1982-83 championship season, scoring 11 points.

Meanwhile, DiNardo was working on his engineering degree when Coach Jim Valvano announced an open tryout in the fall of '82. Since he had been away from the game for a year, DiNardo wasn't sure he could still compete. He called his dad for advice and got it: "If you don't try, you will never know."

WOLFPACK

So he gave it a whirl, competing against two dozen others. He had no idea how he was doing until the last day of camp when assistant coach Ed McLean sauntered up to him and asked him what size shoes he wore (15). He was on the team.

DiNardo rarely played and didn't score a point during his two seasons on the team, but he was part of the national championship. "Tommy was an important part of our team," Valvano said.

And it started with the shoes.

Contemporary society proclaims that it's all about the clothes. Buy that new suit or dress, those new shoes (maybe not size 15's), and all the sparkling accessories, and you'll be a new person. The changes are only cosmetic, though; under those clothes, you're the same person. Consider Joseph, for instance, prancing about in his pretty new clothes; he was still a spoiled little tattletale whom his brothers detested enough to sell into slavery.

Jesus never taught that we should run around half-naked or wear only second-hand clothes from the local mission. He did warn us, though, against making consumer items such as clothes a priority in our lives. A follower of Christ seeks to emulate Jesus not through material, superficial means such as wearing special clothing like a robe and sandals. Rather, the disciple desires to match Jesus' inner beauty and serenity -- whether the clothes the Christian wears are the sables of a king or the rags of a pauper.

It kind of hit me that my dream was coming true.
-- Tommy DiNardo, when asked one size shoes he wore

**Where Jesus is concerned,
clothes don't make the person; faith does.**

IN THE KNOW

Read John 4:19-26, 39-42.

"They said to the woman, . . . 'Now we have heard for ourselves, and we know that this man really is the Savior of the world'" (v. 42).

State linebacker Freddie Aughtry-Lindsay knew quite a few things as he tucked the football under his arm. He knew the home crowd was in a frenzy, that he had a long way to go, and that he had a short time to get there.

On Oct. 11, 2003, the UConn Huskeys showed up for what was one of the most thrilling football games in NC State history. The Pack took a 24-10 with only nine minutes left to play. Quarterback Philip Rivers had two touchdown passes, a 3-yard flip to tailback Cotra Jackson and a 25-yarder to tight end T.J. Williams. Aughtry-Lindsay scored the other Pack touchdown by returning a fumble 48 yards after linebacker Pat Thomas sacked the UConn QB.

To the horror of the Carter-Finley crowd, however, Connecti-cut rallied to tie the game at 24 and then got the ball with 47 seconds left. Rather than deciding to take a knee and send the game into overtime, the Husky coaches opted to try to win it with a hurry-up offense.

UConn moved quickly out to the 42, but then the blitzing Wolf-pack defense pressured the Husky QB into what he later called "a dumb pick." His pass sailed right into Aughtry-Lindsay's welcoming arms. The NC State junior had been a fullback in high school, so he knew a little about running. He also knew the last seconds of the game were ticking away and that if he were tackled after the clock ran out, the game would go into overtime. His goal was the end zone.

He first ran to his right, then cut back to his left, and picked up some blockers. The UConn quarterback grabbed him at the 1, but Aughtry-Lindsay tumbled into the end zone with five seconds left to play. He knew for sure NC State had a win.

They just knew in the same way you know certain things in your life. That your spouse loves you, for instance. That you are good at your job. That tea should be iced and sweetened. That a bad day fishing is still better than a good day at work. That the best barbecue comes from a pig. You know these things even though no mathematician or philosopher can prove any of this on paper.

It's the same way with faith in Jesus: You just know that he is God's son and the savior of the world. You know it in the same way that you know NC State is the only team worth pulling for: with every fiber of your being, with all your heart, your mind, and your soul.

You just know, and because you know him, Jesus knows you. And that is all you really need to know.

I know what I wanna do. What I would like to be able to do is to spend whatever time I have left giving some hope to others.
-- Jim Valvano

A life of faith is lived in certainty and conviction:
You just know you know.

DAY 81

CALLING IT QUITS

Read Numbers 13:25-14:4.

"The men who had gone up with him said, 'We can't attack those people; they are stronger than we are'" (v. 13:31).

One thing you could say about the 1974 Wolfpack football team: They certainly weren't a bunch of quitters.

Lou Holtz's squad made a specialty of coming from behind on its way to a 9-2-1 record. After wins over Wake Forest and Duke, State trailed Clemson 10-9 at the half. For the first time, though, they showed off a characteristic that carried them to a successful season: They refused to quit. The Pack drove 69, 84, and 67 yards in the last half and wound up mauling Clemson 31-10.

Syracuse took a 14-7 lead the following week, but running back Roland Hooks scored three touchdowns and Stan Fritts, whom *USA Today* called the greatest fullback in Wolfpack history, scored another. The Pack won 28-22.

The following week East Carolina led 14-0 before State did it again. Hooks scored two TDs, and Fritts had one in the 24-20 win. Fritts' score was his 36th, a new conference record.

The Wolfpack's sixth straight win featured their biggest comeback yet. Virginia led early on 21-0. This time quarterback Dave Buckey led the rally with a game that earned him National Back of the Week honors. He threw for 306 yards, and ran for a touchdown in the closing minutes in the 22-21 win.

WOLFPACK

The team that refused to quit bounced back from two losses to beat South Carolina, shock No. 1-ranked Penn State 12-7, and bury Arizona State. But they weren't through with their comebacks.

Houston led 31-17 late in the Astro-Bluebonnet Bowl. Tommy Loudon scored on a 9-yard run with 3:33 left, but the two-point try failed. After an onside kick, Buckey led a 47-yard drive. He scored from the one, and Fritts muscled his way in for the two-point conversion. The season ended with a tie and with one more incredible comeback from the team that wouldn't quit.

Remember that time you quit a high-school sports team? Bailed out of a relationship? Walked away from that job with the goals unachieved? Sometimes quitting is the most sensible way to minimize your losses, so you may well at times in your life give up on something or someone.

In your relationship with God, however, you should remember the people of Israel, who quit when the Promised Land was theirs for the taking. They forgot one fact of life you never should: God never gives up on you.

That means you should never, ever give up on God. No matter how tired or discouraged you get, no matter that it seems your prayers aren't getting through to God, no matter what – quitting on God is not an option. He is preparing a blessing for you, and in his time, he will bring it to fruition -- if you don't quit on him.

Don't give up; don't ever give up.
— *Jim Valvano*

Whatever else you give up on in your life, don't give up on God; he will never ever give up on you.

DAY 82

LEGAL THIEVERY

Read Exodus 22:1-15.

"A thief must certainly make restitution" (v. 2b).

Gavin Grant just flat-out stole one for the Pack.

State was 11-5 but was reeling after two straight conference losses when the 14-2, 21st-ranked Miami Hurricanes strode confidently into the RBC Center on Jan. 19, 2008. The Canes faced a hostile crowd of 12,400 on a snowy night. As the game neared its close, though, it was the Pack fans who felt the chill the most.

Everything was nice and warm early on as State jumped out to a 36-27 halftime lead. Miami got hot in the last half, though, and led 72-69 in the last minute. Grant, who scored 14 points in the last 8:31 of regulation, got an old-fashioned three-point play off a fast break to send the game into overtime.

State failed to score on its first six possessions of the OT, and the Canes took advantage. They led 76-72 as the clock rolled under twenty seconds, and the big crowd went silent. Guard Courtney Fells pumped some life into the place by nailing a three with 17.7 seconds left. With 15.3 seconds left, Miami made one of two free throws to lead 77-75.

Grant, who wound up with 22 points, drove the lane to tie it, but missed. Freshman J.J. Hickson was there to follow up and knot the score with only 3.9 seconds left. Both the crowd and the Pack were alive again. "I saw J.J. make the shot and thought, 'It's going to a second overtime and we can win,'" said soph forward

WOLFPACK

Brandon Costner, who scored 16 points. That's what everybody must have thought -- but it's not what happened.

Miami tried a quick inbounds pass to get the ball down court for a game-winner, but the throw went right to Grant instead of the Hurricane he was defending. Quite surprised, Grant nevertheless knew what to do with his steal. He laid it up and in at the buzzer. State had a 79-77 win they had quite literally stolen.

Buckle up your seat belt. Wear a bicycle or motorcycle helmet. Use your pooper scooper to clean up after your dog. Don't walk on the grass. Picky ordinances, picky laws – in all their great abundance, they're an inescapable part of our modern lives.

When Moses came stumbling down Mt. Sinai after spending time as God's secretary, he brought with him a whole mess of laws and regulations, many of which undoubtedly seem picky to us today. What some of them provide, though, are practical examples of what for God is the basic principle underlying the theft of personal property: what is wrong must be made right.

While most of us today probably won't have to worry too much about oxen, sheep, and donkeys, making what is wrong right remains a way of life for Christians. To get right with other people requires anything from restitution to apologies. To get right with God requires Jesus Christ.

He threw it right to me. Right at me. I was like, 'Thanks.'
-- Gavin Grant on his steal

To make right the wrong of stealing
requires restitution; to make right
our relationship with God requires Jesus Christ.

DAY 83

ON THE MONEY

Read Luke 16:1-15.

"You cannot serve both God and money" (v. 13b).

Everett Case unsettled school officials when he took the head coaching job at NC State without even discussing his salary. (See Devotion No. 32.) He wanted the job and that settled it; money was no issue because he had plenty.

"I have been fortunate in my investments," Case told his new bosses in 1946 when they raised the matter of money. They were much more concerned about money than their new basketball coach was, believing that his not having a multiyear contract or a competitive salary would embarrass the school.

But Case told the truth; his dabbling in several businesses and investments had indeed left him with no money worries. While he was coaching high school in Frankfort, Ind., he opened what was called a "California-style drive-in." He sold calendars and various certificates around the state. Both ventures were successful.

Case brought his financial acumen with him to Raleigh. He often tipped his players for running a stock transaction from his office to his stock broker downtown. One investment got away from him, though. In 1959, he sought to bring the first McDonald's to Raleigh. The negotiations broke down, however, when the corporate suits refused to let him call the restaurant "Everett Case's McDonald's."

When he died in 1966, Case left an estate of about a quarter of a million dollars. A lifelong bachelor, he set apart $69,525 to be spread among the 57 living Wolfpack players who had earned their degrees from NC State. That money came in handy for one former player, Bucky Waters, later the head coach at Duke. His son was allergic to milk, so they had to feed him expensive soy milk. "I was making like $5,000 a year," Waters recalled, "and that stuff was 70 cents a can, and he was using three cans a day. So [the money] didn't go into a convertible or anything like that. It was a godsend."

Having too much money at the end of the month is as bothersome -- if not as worrisome -- as having too much month at the end of the money. The investment possibilities are bewildering: stocks, bonds, mutual funds, a McDonald's franchise.

You take your money seriously, as well you should. Jesus, too, took money seriously, warning us frequently of its dangers. Money itself is not evil; its peril lies in the ease with which it can usurp God's rightful place as the master of our lives.

Certainly in our age and society, we often measure people by how much money they have. But like our other talents, gifts, and resources, money should primarily be used for God's purposes. God's love must touch not only our hearts but our wallets also.

How much of your wealth are you investing with God?

Money can buy you everything but happiness. It can pay your fare to everywhere but heaven.

-- *Pete Maravich*

Your attitude about money says much about your attitude toward God.

DAY 84

ANGER MANAGEMENT

Read James 1:19-27.

"Everyone should be quick to listen, slow to speak and slow to become angry, for man's anger does not bring about the righteous life that God desires" (vv. 19-20).

Aghast, horrified, and eerily silent, the NC State crowd was uncertain whether or not it had just witnessed the death of the man many consider the greatest college basketball player ever. And it happened because he got angry.

What has been called "without question . . . the most memorable moment in the first 70 years of the Wolfpack basketball program" occurred on March 16, 1974, in the finals of the Eastern Regionals against Pittsburgh when an angry David Thompson blocked a Panther shot. As he soared as high as he ever did, Thompson's foot caught the shoulder of teammate Phil Spence (who was 6'8" tall). He flipped and landed with his neck perpendicular to his body. He lay unconscious on the floor in twin pools of blood and urine, "a sure sign of a devastating head injury." When teammate Tommy Burleson saw a replay of his friend's injury, he got physically ill.

The play that caused the injury wasn't necessary. Thompson was a "soft-spoken, polite-as-a-preacher young man who never got angry." That afternoon he did, and it cost him. The officials let Pitt slap Thompson on the arm on every shot, and finally he had enough. "He was enraged" and hurried downcourt with only one aim in mind: to block the next Pitt shot. He did and two bad things happened: He was called for goaltending and he was injured.

Despite the horrifying nature of the injury, Thompson played a week later and led the Pack to the national championship. "I got a little upset, which was out of character for me, and I paid a huge price for it," Thompson said about the day he got angry.

Our society today is well aware of anger's destructive power because too many of us don't manage our anger. Anger is a healthy component of a functional human being until – like other normal emotions such as fear, grief, and worry – it escalates out of control. Anger abounds in Raleigh when the Wolfpack lose; the trouble comes when that anger intensifies from annoyance and disappointment to rage and destructive behavior.

Anger has both practical and spiritual consequences. Its great spiritual danger occurs when anger is "a purely selfish matter and the expression of a merely peevish vexation at unexpected and unwelcome misfortune or frustration" as when State commits a turnover in the last minute. It thus interferes with the living of the righteous, Christ-like life God intends for us.

Our own anger, therefore, can incur God's wrath; making God angry can never be anything but a perfectly horrendous idea.

That was a reckless act on my part. That just shows that you shouldn't lose control on the basketball court.
--David Thompson on his injury and the anger that led to it

Anger becomes a problem when it escalates
into rage and interferes with the righteous life
God intends for us.

DAY 85

JUMPING FOR JOY

Read Luke 6:20-26.

"Rejoice in that day and leap for joy, because great is your reward in heaven" (v. 23).

Because Woody Jones could jump, NC State grabbed its first-ever football win over UNC.

When the Wolfpack and the Heels met in 1941, North Carolina had won 11 times and two of the games had ended in ties. On Nov. 11 in Chapel Hill, North Carolina took an early 7-0 lead before State answered on a 1-yard plunge by Art Faircloth. But State missed the extra point, and the 7-6 score stood up into the third quarter.

That's when George W. "Woody" Jones jumped up. Jones was honorable mention All-America in 1941 and a member of State's Southern Conference champion wrestling team in 1941-42. He was also a high jumper on the Wolfpack track team.

In the third quarter, Jones used that jumping ability to block a Carolina punt. "I jumped over the end," he recalled. "He thought we were coming in low." Jones called the blocked punt "the best kiss I ever had. I got it [the ball] partly with my hand and my face." Because he had broken his nose earlier, Jones was the only State player that day wearing a face mask.

Jones fell on the loose ball to set up one of the most famous runs in State history. Coach Doc Newton's Pack ran a single wing offense in 1941 with the quarterback, co-captain Bob Cathey, in a crouch behind the center. The quarterback for the most part was a blocking back, so Cathey rarely ran the ball. But on second down from the 16 after Jones' block, Cathey ran a "quarterback sneak." He took the ball from center Jimmy Allen, faked a handoff, tucked the ball into his stomach, bent over, and moved slowly down the field. He scored virtually untouched for the 13-7 Pack win, a run set up because Woody Jones could jump.

You're probably a pretty good jumper yourself when State scores against UNC. You just can't help it. It's like your feet and your seat have suddenly become magnets that repel each other. The sad part is that you always come back down to earth; the moment of exultation passes.

But what if you could jump for joy all the time? Not literally, of course; you'd pass out from exhaustion. But figuratively, with your heart aglow and joyous even when life is its most difficult.

Joy is an absolutely essential component of the Christian life. Not only do we experience joy in our public praise and worship – which is temporary – but we live daily in the joy that comes from the presence of God in our lives and the surety of his saving power extended to us through Jesus Christ.

It's not happiness, which derives from external factors; it's joy, which comes from inside.

It was the highlight of the year. The whole student body went crazy.
-- Woody Jones on the 1941 win over UNC

Unbridled joy can send you jumping all over the place; life in Jesus means such exultation is not rare but rather is a way of life.

UNBELIEVABLE

Read Hebrews 3:7-19.

"See to it, brothers, that none of you has a sinful, unbelieving heart that turns away from the living God" (v. 12).

Here's what it would take for State to win: a storybook finish, an unforgettable play, a last-gasp pass thrown by a hometown kid making his first college start. In other words, it would take something downright unbelievable. But that's what happened.

On Sept. 23, 2006, 1-2 NC State hosted the 20th-ranked Boston College Eagles. The game seemed to unfold as everyone expected when BC scored with 12:55 left to lead 15-10 and then intercepted a pass at the Wolfpack 35 with only 3:08 to play. But the NC State defense refused to concede; BC couldn't make a first down and didn't even try a field goal.

Still, that left the Pack with the ball at its own 28 with only 46 seconds left, no timeouts, and redshirt sophomore Daniel Evans at quarterback. Many of the Wolfpack faithful had probably right about now lost a great deal of their faith.

They shouldn't have. Looking like a fifth-year senior, Evans completed three of four passes, including a 20-yard sideline toss to junior wide receiver John Dunlap. With 16.8 ticks on the clock, the Pack sat at the Eagle 34. That's when something unbelievable happened.

Evans pump-faked and moved to his right. He then gunned

the ball to the end zone where Dunlap leaped for the ball over a shorter cornerback. He bobbled the ball but pulled it in and held on as he hit the turf. Touchdown! State wins!

"It's an amazing feeling," Evans said. "To win a game, not only to win it but to win it like we did, is just amazing." It's also unbelievable.

What we claim not to believe in reveals much about us. UFOs. Global warming. Sasquatch. Aluminum baseball bats and the designated hitter.

Most of what passes for our unbelief has little effect on our lives. Does it matter much that we don't believe a Ginsu knife can stay sharp after repeatedly slicing through tin cans? Or that any other team besides NC State is worth pulling for?

That's not the case, however, when Jesus and God are part of the mix. Quite unbelievably, we often hear people blithely assert they don't believe in God. Or brazenly declare they believe in God but don't believe Jesus was anything but a good man and a great teacher.

At this point, unbelief becomes dangerous because God doesn't fool around with scoffers. He locks them out of the Promised Land, which isn't a country in the Middle East but Heaven itself.

Given that scenario, it's downright unbelievable that anyone would not believe.

They never stopped believing.
-- State head coach Chuck Amato after the win over BC

Perhaps nothing is as unbelievable as that some people insist on not believing in God or his son.

DAY 87

THE FAME GAME

Read 1 Kings 10:1-10, 18-29.

"King Solomon was greater in riches and wisdom than all the other kings of the earth. The whole world sought audience with Solomon" (vv. 23-24).

Lorenzo Charles remains deservedly famous for his buzzer-beating dunk that beat Houston for the 1983 national championship. Actually, though, he was a much better basketball player his last two seasons at State than he was as a sophomore.

In fact, Charles didn't have a very good game in those finals. He scored only four points including that one famous dunk. Reserve forward Mike Warren noticed the lack of Charles' specialty. As the last timeout ended, he grabbed Charles and said, "Lo, you don't have any dunks yet; that's why we're struggling. You've got to get a dunk to win the game."

Charles "used to try to dunk everything," Jim Valvano said. "A little child walked by, and he tried to dunk him." As he saw little action that magical season until Derek Whittenburg broke a foot in January, Charles wasn't really in good shape. "There were times," Valvano said, "when he couldn't run up and down the court three times without asking to be taken out."

The fame of THE shot spurred Charles to get into the weight room for the first time after his sophomore season. The result was a body that earned him the nickname "Lorilla" from his teammates and his becoming a fearsomely strong offensive player as a junior. One coach said Charles was so strong he had to promise his players' mothers he wouldn't make their sons guard him.

Charles completed the less-famous part of his State career as a two-time first-team All-ACC player.

Have you ever wanted to be famous? Hanging out with other rich and famous people, having folks with microphones listen to what you say, throwing money around like toilet paper, meeting adoring and clamoring fans, signing autographs, and posing for the paparazzi before you climb into your imported sports car?

Many of us yearn to be famous, well-known in the places and by the people that we believe matter. That's all fame amounts to: strangers knowing your name and your face.

The truth is that you are already famous where it really does matter, which excludes TV's talking heads, screaming teenagers, rapt moviegoers, or D.C. power brokers. You are famous because Almighty God knows your name, your face, and everything about you.

If a persistent photographer snapped you pondering this fame – the only kind that has eternal significance – would the picture show the world unbridled joy or the shell-shocked expression of a mug shot?

More than 20 years later, people are still talking about it. I thought I would have my little 15 minutes of fame and that would be it.
– Lorenzo Charles

You're already famous because God knows your name and your face, which may be either reassuring or terrifying.

DAY 88

WHO, ME?

Read Judges 6:11-23.

"'But Lord,' Gideon asked, 'how can I save Israel? My clan is the weakest in Manasseh, and I am the least in my family'" (v. 15).

Six games into the 1967-68 season, Vann Williford was a starter, which was "a big surprise for everybody, including Williford." After all, he was a recruit virtually nobody wanted.

Williford dreamed of playing at Reynolds Coliseum for years, but his "spindly frame" led practically all the colleges to overlook the 6'6" forward. He ended up committing to Pfeiffer University with the clear understanding that he would go somewhere else if he got a better offer.

Events conspired to make that happen. NC State coach Press Maravich had no interest in Williford because he had a star forward already lined up: his son, Pete. But when the son didn't make enough on his SAT's to get into State, father and son took off for LSU prior to the 1966-67 season. (See Devotion No. 77.)

When new head coach Norm Sloan arrived, he realized he needed some players since Maravich had signed only one recruit. Sloan asked about unsigned players, and a booster sent him an eight-millimeter film of a Williford game. Based solely on that grainy film (and on a measure of desperation), Sloan offered Williford a scholarship. The youngster was so eager to sign that he interrupted Sloan in the middle of a golf game to seal the deal.

Williford struggled as a freshman, and Sloan openly discussed redshirting him as a sophomore. But Williford worked on his game over the summer, and his skills fit perfectly into Sloan's offense. Early in the 1967-68 season, he became a surprise starter. In fact, Williford was so surprised and so nervous about his debut that he put his gym shorts on backwards in the locker room.

The total surprise of a starter was first-team All-ACC in 1969 and '70 and the ACC Tournament MVP in 1970.

No doubt you've experienced that moment of unwelcome surprise with its sinking "who, me?" feeling, which is usually not as pleasant as Vann Williford's was. How about that time the teacher called on you when you hadn't done a lick of homework? Or the night the hypnotist pulled you out of the audience to be his guinea pig? You've had the wide-eyed look and the turmoil in your midsection when you were suddenly singled out and found yourself in a situation you neither sought nor were prepared for.

That "who, me" feeling applies especially to being called to serve God in some way. As Gideon did when God tapped him, you may quail at being audacious enough to teach Sunday school, lead a small group study, or coordinate a high school prayer club. After all, who's worthy enough to do anything like that?

The truth is that nobody is – but that doesn't seem to matter to God. And it's his opinion, not yours, that counts.

Surprise me.
-- Yogi Berra on where his wife should have him buried

You're right in that no one is worthy to serve God,
but the problem is that doesn't matter to God.

TEAM PLAYERS

Read 1 Corinthians 12:4-13; 27-31.

"Now to each one the manifestation of the Spirit is given for the common good" (v. 7).

North Carolina State athletic director Lee Fowler didn't just get a basketball coach when he hired Kellie Harper; he got a team.

In the spring of 2009, Fowler's negotiations with Harper to bring her aboard as State's third-ever women's basketball coach hit a snag when Harper insisted that her husband, Jon, come with her from Western Carolina as an assistant coach.

The Harpers are a team. Jon was a manager of the women's basketball team at Auburn when he met and started dating Kellie Jolly, the star point guard on three Tennessee national championship team from 1995-99. After they married in 1999, they decided to forge a coaching path together.

Kellie got the first head-coaching opportunity, Western Carolina in 2004, with Jon as her assistant. Then came the State offer. "I felt like it had to be done," Kellie said about negotiating for her husband to join her. "We've got something that works."

The university's nepotism policy, however, flatly forbids such an arrangement, so Fowler and the school chancellor worked out the details that let it all happen. Jon would be a non-paid assistant who would be reimbursed for basketball-related expenses and would be allowed to earn income from summer camps.

The Harpers admittedly work hard to shield their relationship in public. "They hardly show affection," State junior Tia Bell noticed. "You don't really see them hugging. Definitely not kissing. It's a coach and an assistant." Once when they went to the movies together, the players teased them with "Ah, that's so cute."

"I don't know how they do it," remarked L'Tona Lamonte, State's director of women's basketball operations about the Harpers' unusual team coaching arrangement. They do, though.

Most accomplishments are the result of teamwork, whether it's a college basketball team, the running of a household, a project at work, or a dance recital. Disparate talents and gifts work together for the common good and the greater goal.

A church works exactly the same way. At its most basic, a church is a team assembled by God. A shared faith drives the team members and impels them toward shared goals. As a successful basketball team must have guards and forwards, so must a church be composed of people with different spiritual and personal gifts. The result is something greater than everyone involved.

What makes a church team different from others is that the individual efforts are expended for the glory of God and not self. The nature of a church member's particular talents doesn't matter; what does matter is that those talents are used as part of God's team.

It works for us.
— Kellie Harper on their unusual working arrangement

A church is a team of people using their various talents and gifts for God, the source of all those abilities to begin with.

DAY 90

GOOD-BYE AGAIN

Read John 13:33-38.

"My children, I will be with you only a little longer" (v. 33a).

State said good-bye to its first on-campus gymnasium by playing a game fans weren't allowed to see.

North Carolina A&M played its first basketball game (See Devotion No. 1.) in Pullen Hall in 1910, but held its subsequent contests at Raleigh's Municipal Auditorium, which "barely had enough room for a basketball court." In March 1923, the Board of Trustees announced that a gym would be built and would be named after Frank Thompson, a State college athlete and Wake Forest coach who had been killed in World War I.

Construction of Thompson Gym began in November 1923. The gym seated about 4,000 with some additional standing room. The first contest against outside competition occurred on Dec. 19, 1924, when the Farmers took on the Durham Elks team. State captain Red Johnson scored the first basket, and the Raleigh boys jumped out to a 29-8 lead. At that point, the Elks coach pulled his team from the court, alleging unfairness by the lone referee and thus ending the game with fourteen minutes left to play. The first intercollegiate game in the facility was a 29-22 win over Duke.

Thompson gym served State well for 24 seasons; the Wolfpack had a record of 189-92 there. Finally, though, basketball at the college got too big for the building. A game against UNC during the 1946-47 season was cancelled because of the overflow crowd. The following season, the Duke game was postponed when fire officials condemned the building for having insufficient exits.

Fans weren't even allowed to say good-bye to the gym. Its basketball days ended rather ignominiously on Jan. 23, 1948, with a game against High Point College. No fans were allowed in the building because of the ongoing condemnation by fire officials.

You've stood on the curb and watched someone you love drive off, or you've grabbed a last-minute hug before a plane leaves. Maybe it was a child leaving home for the first time or your best friends moving halfway across the country. It's an extended – maybe even permanent – separation, and good-byes hurt.

Jesus felt the pain of parting too. Throughout his brief ministry, Jesus had been surrounded by and had depended upon his friends and confidants, the disciples. About to leave them, he gathered them for a going-away supper and gave them a heads-up about what was about to happen. In the process, he offered them words of comfort. What a wonderful friend he was! Even though he was the one who was about to suffer unimaginable agony, Jesus' concern was for the pain his friends would feel.

But Jesus wasn't just saying good-bye. He was on his mission of providing the way through which none of us would ever have to say good-bye again.

They say money talks. The only thing it says to me is good-bye.
— Baseball Hall of Famer Paul Waner

Through Jesus, we will see the day
when we say good-bye to good-byes.

NOTES
(by Devotion Day Number)

1   a group of students petitioned . . . to field a team.: Thad Mumau, *Go Wolf-pack* (Huntsville, AL: The Strode Publishers, 1981), p. 27.

1   The school received some . . . so they could practice.: Mumau, p. 29.

1   A&M had some students . . . team in 1890 and '91.: Mumau, pp. 27, 29.

2   the students paid athletic . . . ran the association.: Douglas Herakovich, *Wolfpack Handbook* (Wichita, KS: The Wichita Eagle and Beacon Publishing Co., 1996), pp. 6-7.

2   the association in 1910 . . . games against Wake Forest.: Herakovich, p. 7.

2   a floor that was rendered slick by a dance the night before: Herakovich, p. 8.

2   The names of G.K. Bryan . . . at their Alma Mater.: Herakovich, p. 6.

3   "He had no family, . . . greatest game ever invented.": Herakovich, p. 24.

3   "to start a new legend and a new religion.: Herakovich, p. 24.

3   He accepted the head . . . isn't the big consideration.: Tim Peeler, *Legends of N.C. State Basketball* (Champaign, IL: Sports Publishing L.L.C., 2004), p. 4.

3   "the hulking skeleton of. . . recruiting, coaching, and promoting.": Peeler, p. 5.

3   "Carolina and Duke and . . . to improve (because of Case,": Peeler, p. 6.

3   He introduced the Indiana . . . that shows player stats.: Peeler, p. 7.

3   He is the one who brought basketball to the ACC.: Peeler, p. 9.

4   When he was 2, his dad, . . . some slow, white farm kid,": J.P. Giglio, "State's Sure Shot," *The News & Observer*, Jan. 20, 2010.

4   Sidney Lowe called him a "throwback.": Giglio, "State's Sure Shot."

5   Jim Valvano, however, used . . . fearsome fast break.: Herakovich, p. 126.

5   Valvano wanted his team . . . and create a shot.: Herakovich, p. 127.

5   "I was . . . exactly where . . . a decent offensive rebounder.": Peeler, *Legends of N.C. State Basketball*, p. 130.

5   I was in the wrong place at the right time.: Peeler, *Legends of N.C. State Basketball*, p. 130.

6   Dave and Don Buckey admitted . . . on an airplane before.: Mumau, p. 131.

6   "We had decided to go . . . Mid-American Conference.": Mumau, p. 130.

6   Purdue made a weak . . . Rein had changed schools.: Mumau, pp. 130-31.

6   "Don and I were just . . . rest of the Buckey family.: Mumau, p. 131.

6   We did everything together, . . . did admire each other.: Mumau, p. 131.

7   "rugged, gritty contests.": Chip Alexander, "The Pack Is Back." *The News & Observer.* March 10, 2002, p. C1, http://nl.newsbank.com/nl-search/we/Archives?p_action=print&p_docid=0F22F913056B7, Aug. 17, 2010.

7   State went into its spread . . . get the shot off, quick.": Alexander, "The Pack Is Back."

8   Horvath was a 6-6 native . . . and threw it out.": Herakovich, p. 47.

8   Case sent Horvath another . . . a visit and a tryout.: Herakovich, pp. 47-48.

8   Horvath didn't toss that . . . come on down and play;: Herakovich, p. 48.

8   It wasn't long before . . . hadn't found my life's work.: Herakovich, p. 48.

9   "David Thompson is the . . . ever in college basketball.": Peeler, p. 86.

9   offended that the ACC . . . its greatest athlete ever.: Peeler, p. 86.

9 late in his final home game, . . . great way to end my career,": Peeler, p. 88.
9 He left State in the spring of 1975 . . . stage that December.: Peeler, p. 88.
9 Thompson's home is filled . . . It completes me.": Peeler, p. 89.
9 It was something that bothered me for a lot of years.: Peeler, p. 88.
10 she learned that her players . . . learned they were competitive.: "A Coach's First Season," *gopack.com*, April 6, 2010, http://www.gopack.com/sports/ w-baskbl/spec-rel/040610aaa.html, Aug. 9, 2010.
10 "or some kind of medieval stretching device,": Tim Peeler, "Intense Workouts Prepares [*sic*] Women's Basketball for Upcoming Season," *gopack.com*, Aug. 9, 2010, http://www.gopack.com/sports/w-baskbl/spec-rel/080910aae. html, Aug. 9, 2010.
10 So at 6. a.m., shortly . . . have to be strong,": Peeler, "Intense Workouts."
10 We want to be the . . . physical than they are.: Peeler, Intense Workouts."
11 Even as late as 1950, . . . among his starters.: Herakovich, p. 29.
11 He and assistant coach . . . almost every vacant lot.": Herakovich, p. 29.
12 "If we had lost . . . a shot at the NCAA,": Tim Peeler, *When March Went Mad* (Champaign, IL: Sports Publishing L.L.C., 2007), p. 186.
12 Coach Jim Valvano had it . . the State-Wake game. Peeler, *When March Went Mad*, p. 185.
12 The team was still in Atlanta . . . somewhere in Atlanta?": Peeler, *When March Went Mad*, pp. 190-91.
13 the job didn't pay much, . . . her old one to her mother.: Mechelle Voepel, "Yow's Considerable Efforts Will Live On," *ESPN.com*, Jan. 24, 2009, http: //sports.espn.go.com.ncw/columns/story?columnist=voepel_mechelle&id= 3853652, Aug. 13, 2010.
13 "Everyone feels a connection . . . being, first and foremost.": Voepel.
13 State wrestling coach Carter . . . learning of her death.: A.J. Carr, "'She's in a Better Place,'" *The News & Observer*, Jan. 25, 2009.
13 "beacon of hope and determination and love and joy": Carr, "'She's in a Better Place.'"
13 "First and foremost she was a Christian,": Carr, "'She's in a Better Place.'"
13 I know she's in . . . going to miss her.: Carr, "'She's in a Better Place.'"
14 State was hit a good bit . . . with a similar predicament: Herakovich, p. 22.
15 Before each season, he . . . can't play basketball for me.": Peeler, p. 56.
15 In a book, he openly . . . for his dorm deposit.: Peeler, p. 57.
15 primarily concerned with . . . to recruit a player.: Peeler, pp. 57-58.
15 "But to me," he said, . . . should be taken care,: Peeler, p. 58.
15 We took a bad lick. . . . to what goes on today.: Peeler, p. 58.
16 During the summer of 2008, . . . including the Olympics.: Carr, A.J., "Heart of a Champion," *The News & Observer*, March 29, 2009, Aug. 12, 2010.
16 I'm glad I came back . . . could achieve this here.": Carr, "Heart of a Champion."
17 "Why are you going to . . . right in your backyard?": Herakovich, p. 110.
17 "If you go pro, . . . And time will run out,": Herakovich, p. 111.
18 It arose out of an evening . . . attended the first tournament.: Herakovich, pp. 52-53.
18 The Classic was a rarity . . . make money on basketball.: Herakovich, p. 54.
18 The visiting teams were formally welcomed at the airport:

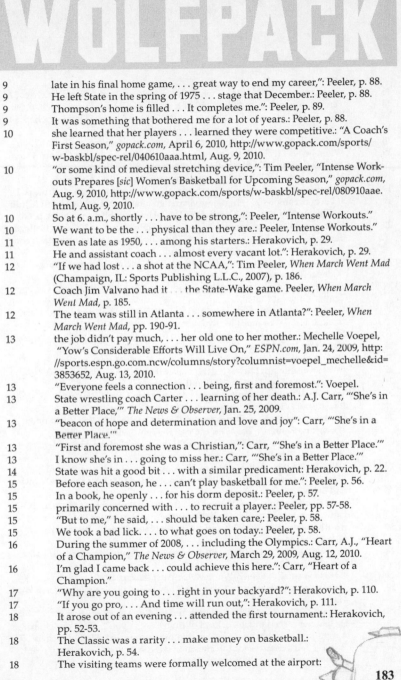

Herakovich, p. 53.

18   were the guests of honor . . . whole town was involved.": Herakovich, p. 52.

18   Penn State coach John Egli . . . what team he plays for.": Herakovich, p. 54.

18   The last Dixie Classic, . . . almost $21,000 plus expenses.: Herakovich, p. 54.

18   made the Classic an easy target.: Herakovich, p. 55.

18   A glorious 12-year tradition became a memory.: Herakovich, p. 55.

19   When he was 17, Jim Valvao wrote down his life's goal.: Bob Cairns, *V & Me* (Alexander, NC: Alexander Books, 2005), p. 21.

19   Valvano was so dedicated . . . know lobsters had tails!": Cairns, p. 22.

19   Valvano wrote those goals . . . win an NCAA championship.: Cairns, p. 21.

19   If I ever accomplish . . . higher goal and go after that.: Bettinger, Jim & Julie S., The Book of Bowden (Nashville: TowleHouse Publishing, 2001), p. 66.

20   Sadri strode onto the tennis . . . and a red State blazer.: A.J. Carr, "College Tennis' Greatest Match," *gopack.com*, July 31, 2010, http://www.gopack.com/sports/m-tennis-spec-rel/073110aaa.html, Aug. 2, 2010.

20   "was drenched with drama, . . . [the players'] racquet strings.": Carr, "College Tennis' Greatest Match."

20   Aware of McEnroe's propensity . . . not going to take this.: Carr, "College Tennis' Greatest Match."

20   [McEnroe] was a great player, [but] I really felt I was going to win.: Carr, "Collge Tennis' Greatest Match."

21   No way am I going to . . . eaten alive in the ACC.": Peeler, p. 93.

21   Sloan was looking for . . . the player was only 5'7" tall: Peeler, p. 93.

21   Dickey reminded the coach . . . recommended sight unseen.: Peeler, p. 93.

21   "We never thought [Towe] . . . the player that he was,": Peeler, p. 93.

21   the "heart and soul" of the national champions.: Peeler, p. 92.

21   Towe and David Thompson are . . . a pretty good play.": Peeler, p. 96.

21   It was pretty clear that . . . very close to No. 6.: Peeler, p. 92.

22   "smashed the Pack . . . Burleson and Chris Corchiani," Chip Alexander, "Lowe and Behold," *The News & Observer*, Feb. 4, 2007.

22   left Williams fuming as he . . . brought the house down.: Alexander, "Lowe and Behold."

22   "We wanted it more than they did,": Alexander, "Lowe and Behold."

22   They had more passion . . . I'll never understand that.: Alexander, "Lowe and Behold."

23   "was floundering in mediocrity." . . . thirteen scholarships.: Mumau, p. 42.

23   I always thought I could . . . challenge there was at State.: Mumau, p. 41.

24   was the same as every . . . I could play for Notre Dame,": Peeler, *When March Went Mad*, p. 127.

24   He even had dinner with . . . Rudy wore in that game.: Peeler, *When March Went Mad*, p. 128.

24   "He is too small.": Peeler, *When March Went Mad*, p. 128.

24   A career in broadcasting . . . you don't have one.": Peeler, *When March Went Mad*, p. 139.

25   he was leaning toward . . . a chance and he did.: Herakovich, p. 39.

25   He had not played much . . . kind of tubby, aren't you?": Herakovich, p. 39.

25   A tight-knit bunch who . . . best guard in the country.": Herakovich, p. 39.

26   "We felt Ted's chances for the Heisman were very good,": Mumau, p. 161.

26   "He got banged up.": Mumau, p. 161.

26   Two knee injuries and a shoulder injury: Mumau, p. 162.

26   Brown didn't plan to . . . made for the circumstances.: Mumau, 164.

26   For any running back to be . . . no fun to be hurt.: Mumau, p. 163.

27   Early on, Worsley played very . . . he didn't shoot more.: Herakovich, p. 80.

27   Duke coach Vic Bubas used . . . I might be it.": Herakovich, p. 80.

27   I never had any idea . . . That's all I cared about.: Herakovich, p. 80.

28   Davis was the starting . . . lasted only two series.: Chip Alexander, "Post-game Report," *The News & Observer*, Oct. 3, 2004, http://nl.newsbank.com/nl-search/we/Archives?p_action=print&p_docid=1057F4780EE54, Aug. 19, 2010.

28   hitting 3-of-6 passes for a paltry 19 yards.: Caulton Tudor, "Davis Heats Up Just in Time to Save Pack's Day," *The News & Observer*, Oct. 3, 2004, http://nl.newsbank.com/nl-search/we/Archives?p_action=print&p_docid=1057F477FB889, Aug. 19, 2010.

28   who played the rest of the half.: Alexander, "Postgame Report."

28   "I was not upset . . . Jay, you're in.": Alexander, "Postgame Report."

28   "One play sparked it all,": Alexander, "Postgame Report."

28   "At halftime I would have started you [at quarterback],": Tudor: "Davis Heats Up."

28   We were looking for anything to spark us.: Alexander, "Postgame Report."

29   Sims followed in her older . . . keeps hitters off balance.": Rachel Carter, "State's Strong Arm," *The News & Observer*, May 10, 2007.

29   It took the coach a minute . . . mentioning the perfect game.: Carter, "State's Strong Arm."

29   It's a great feeling. It's kind of an out-of-body experience.: Carter, "State's Strong Arm."

30   As a freshman he assisted . . . maybe not quite so loud.": Robbi Pickeral, "Mock Went Both Ways in Rivalry," *The News & Observer*, March 10, 2009.

30   I felt sort of funny . . . against my former teammates.: Pickeral.

31   Norm Sloan ordered the Pack . . . He never did.": Herakovich, p. 87

31   Bubas left Lewis under . . . too quick for his team.: Herakovich, pp. 87-88.

31   Kretzer dribbled most of the half away;: Herakovich, p. 88.

31   every time Sloan talked to . . . trotted over, too,: Herakovich, p. 88.

31   leading Biedenback to suggest they call a time out.: Herakovich, pp. 88-89.

31   "If we call time-out, . . . put in a real player,": Herakovich, p. 89.

31   He told his team to start playing.: Herakovich, p. 88.

31   There was no grand strategy . . . to stay in a zone.: Herakovich, p. 88.

32   We're never going to get . . . know anybody in Denver.": Peeler, p. 35.

32   "first true superstar." . . . this kid is worth a look.": Peeler, p. 35.

32   expected to settle there.: Peeler, p. 35.

32   Shavlik realized he wanted . . . the campus and the people,: Peeler, p. 36.

32   "despicable, vile, unprincipled scoundrels.": John MacArthur, *Twelve Ordinary Men* (Nashville: W Publishing Group, 2002), p. 152.

32   We won't get him if we don't try.: Peeler, p. 36.

33   Thompson calls the "unsung hero" . . . He was kind of the enforcer,": A.J. Carr, "'74 Players Sing Each Other's Praises," *The News & Observer*, Dec. 23, 2008.

33   "My role has always . . . That's fine with me.": Carr, "'74 Players Sing."

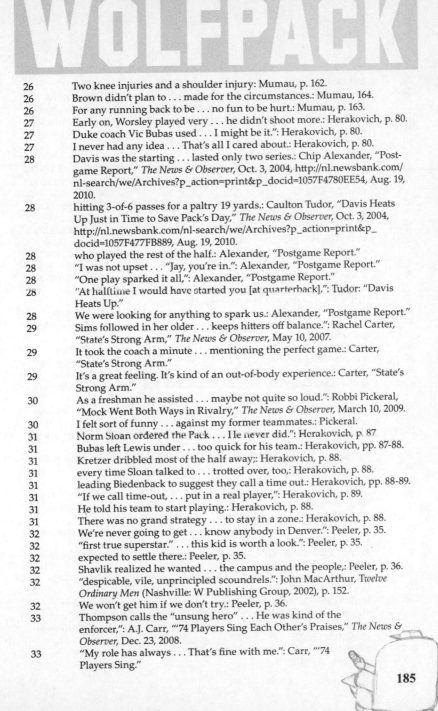

33   as he travels as a . . . still ask him about it.: Carr, "'74 Players Sing."

34   disparage him as an "ugly duckling.": Chip Alexander, "Throwing His Own Way," *The News & Observer*, Aug. 24, 2002, http://nl.newsbank.com/nl-search/we/Archives?p_action=print&p_docid=0F59F999A38A, Aug. 18, 2010.

34   "unorthodox, slightly sidearm . . . the hand to the man.": Alexander, "Throwing His Own Way."

34   It's almost like my trademark now.: Alexander, "Throwing His Own Way."

35   "It's the best job defensively we have ever done,": Peeler, *When March Went Mad*, p. 147.

35   in frustration during a time out, . . . was a total blank.": Peeler, *When March Went Mad*, p. 148.

36   He had never kicked . . . to let him try a 36-yarder.: Jim Sumner, "Looking Back: The 1957 NC State Football Team's Run to the ACC Crown," *TheACC.com*, Oct. 10, 2007, http://www.theacc.com/sports/m-footbl/spec-rel/101007aaa.html, Aug. 5, 2010.

36   It was the greatest day I've ever had on a football field.: Sumner, "Looking Back: The 1957 NC State Football Team's Run to the ACC Crown."

37   There wasn't a dry eye in the place.": Herakovich, p. 76.

37   After a loss to Wake . . . Bryant as his assistant.: Herakovich, pp. 75-76.

37   Case formally announced his . . . not the proper thing to do.": Herakovich, p. 76.

37   punched him on the shoulder . . . strand of the net.: Herakovich, p. 76.

37   "You talk about symbolism . . . a dry eye in the place.": Herakovich, p. 76.

38   "the most dramatic, spine-tingling play": Chip Alexander, "'We Make Games Exciting': McCauley's Slam Downs Deacons," *The News & Observer*, Feb. 4, 2008.

38   "I was thinking, 'Gavin . . . as the buzzer sounded: Alexander, "'We Make Games Exciting.'"

38   He caught it off the rim something vicious.: Alexander, "'We Make Games Exciting."

39   "When you get the chance . . . kind of personality he had,": Mumau, p. 140.

39   "everyone was jumping up and down": Mumau, p. 142.

39   It's like a death in the family.: p. 175.

40   They're used to losing.": Chip Alexander, "An Oh-So-Sweet Sunday," *The News & Observer*, March 21, 2005, http://nl.newsbank.com/nl-search/we/Archives?p_action=print&p_docid=1-8FC9A484ED, Aug. 19, 2010.

40   "Oh, man, that was crazy," . . . "Pride, respect, payback.": Alexander, "An Oh-So-Sweet Sunday."

40   Junior forward Ilian Evtimov . . . from center Jordan Collins,: Alexander, "An Oh-So-Sweet Sunday."

40   a last-second, desperate Husky heave clanked off the front rim.: Alexander, "An Oh-So-Sweet Sunday."

41   In 1968, only the ACC champion . . . drove in three runs: Jim Sumner, "Looking Back: NC State's Road to Omaha 40 Years Ago," *The ACC.com*, April 30, 2008. http://www.theacc.com/sports/m-basebl/spec-rel/043008aaa.html, Aug. 5, 2010.

41   We overachieved. . . . people picked us up.: Sumner, "Looking Back: NC State's Road to Omaha."

186

42   "may have been the second . . . behind David [Thompson].": Peeler, *Legends of N.C. State Basketball*, p. 101.

42   was "ahead of his time." . . . and take jump shots.": Peeler, *Legends of N.C. State Basketball*, p. 102.

42   had declared the Olympics . . . "fun I have ever had.": Peeler, *Legends of N.C. State Basketball*, 103.

42   Smith required that all his . . . Carr on his second attempt.: Peeler, *Legends of N.C. State Basketball*, p. 103.

42   It was a mental thing. I just hated it.: Peeler, *Legends of N.C. State Basketball*, p. 103.

43   Prior to the 1937-38 basketball season, . . . played on a banked court.": Herakovich, p. 19.

43   Coach Ray Sermon had six . . . Iron Five soldiered on,: Herakovich, p. 19.

43   sometimes playing games . . . down with an injury.: Herakovich, pp. 19-20.

43   "They are the fightingest bunch of kids I ever saw,": Herakovich, p. 20.

43   They're fighting their hearts . . . in there on their nerve.: Herakovich, p. 20.

44   O'Brien doesn't like his quarterbacks . . . How can they?": Chip Alexander, "O'Brien's Approach: Keep It Simple, State," *The News & Observer*, Aug. 10, 2007.

44   "Our coaches know about . . . to do outside football,": Alexander, "O'Brien's Approach."

44   not ending practices with . . . players to the Murphy Center.: Alexander, "O'Brien's Approach."

44   "There were a lot of plays, . . . being able to execute the offense,": Alexander, "O'Brien's Approach."

44   It's just simple. You get . . . want to fight anymore.": Alexander, "O'Brien's Approach."

45   Following the season, Case . . . professional team in Louisville,: Herakovich, p. 39.

45   he had "found a few . . . who helped him recruit.: Herakovich, p. 40.

45   Wake Memorial Church had . . . him at the banquet.: Herakovich, p. 40.

45   After being with those kids . . . was no place for me.: Herakovich, p. 40.

46   Valvano had a lineup that simply . . . a calmness to the team.": Jim Sumner, "Looking Back: NC State's Legendary ACC Tournament Title," *TheACC.com*, March 7, 2007, http://www.theacc.com/sports/m-baskbl/specrel/030707aaf.html, Aug. 5, 2010.

46   "The enormity of winning . . . That way it was manageable.": Jim Sumner, "Looking Back: NC State's Legendary ACC Tournament Title."

46   UNC had seven future NBA players: Jim Sumner, "Looking Back: NC State's Legendary ACC Tournament Title."

46   You're never out of it in this league.: Jim Sumner, "Looking Back: NC State's Legendary ACC Tournament Title."

47   when he played a home . . . I couldn't read it,": Herakovich, p. 81.

47   As he brought the ball . . . "I was mighty embarrassed,": Herakovich, p. 81.

47   Afterward, it was funny, . . . wasn't funny at all.: Herakovich, p. 81.

48   "Two-a-days are tough . . . He'll wear you down.": Lorenzo Perez, "After Baby-Sitting, Two-a-Days Not So Daunting," *The News & Observer*, July 16, 2006.

49   She didn't want him playing . . . Washington, D.C., suburb.:

Peeler, *When March Went Mad*, p. 31.

49 He went along with her . . . giving basketball a try.: Peeler, *When March Went Mad*, p. 33.

49 who twice cut him from . . . quit wasting his time.": Peeler, *When March Went Mad*, p. 31.

49 getting to school . . . work on his game.: Peeler, *When March Went Mad*, p. 34.

49 "Norm wasn't sold on him at all,": Peeler, *When March Went Mad*, p. 31.

49 He also created an iconic . . . win over North Carolina.: Peeler, *When March Went Mad*, p. 30.

49 Coach Jim Valvano had to beg the Utah Jazz to draft Bailey.: Peeler, *When March Went Mad*, p. 36.

49 [The coach who told him . . . and what I wanted.: Peeler, *When March Went Mad*, p. 31.

50 about a hundred students . . . both in and atop cars.: Herakovich, p. 16.

50 starting all over again . . . than to be governor.": Herakovich, pp. 16-17.

50 The final buzzer set off . . . campus back in Raleigh.: Herakovich, p. 16.

51 "arguably the Wolfpack's top defender in 2008.": Heather Dinich, "Irving Won't Be Limited in Practice," *ESPN.com*, Feb. 26, 2010, http://sports.espn.go.com/ncf/news/story?id=4948979, Aug. 2, 2010.

51 "Instinctively, Nate's the best defensive player I've been around.": Jim Henry, "N.C. State's Nate Irving Thankful for Second Chance -- at Life and Football," *fanhouse.com*, July 6, 2010, http://ncaafootball.fanhouse.com/2010/07/06, July 7, 2010.

51 Irving visited his family . . . with tears in their eyes.: Henry.

51 "knows he's lucky to be alive.": John Taylor, "It's a Miracle NC State LB Nate Irving Is Still Amongst the Living," *nbcsports.com*, July 25. 1010, http://collegefootballtalk.nbcsports.com/2010/07/25, Aug. 2, 2010.

51 I thought I was . . . matured a lot in my decision-making,": Henry.

51 There's nothing more important . . . I didn't get enough rest.: Henry.

52 Six of the players . . . drafted by the NBA.: Herakovich, p. 99.

52 "the greatest individual performance . . . played in ACC history.": Peeler, *Legends of N.C. State Basketball*, p. 74.

52 "That's the greatest game . . . win the whole thing,": Herakovich, p. 101.

53 the squad played thirty road games before it ever played at home.: Al Myatt, "Finally, a Real Home Game," *The News & Observer*, April 2, 2003, http://nl.newsbank.com/nl-search/we/Archives?p_action=print&p_docid=0FA2B0D85C04, Aug. 19, 2010.

53 the seventh site where . . . high school fields for practice.: Myatt.

53 seating was limited to . . . admission was free.: Myatt.

53 Personally, I love road trips.: Myatt.

54 Man, how big is your playbook?" . . . the line of scrimmage,": Caulton Tudor, "From the Bag of Tricks," *The News & Observer*, Jan. 2, 2003, http://nl.newsbank.com/nl-search/we/Archives?p_action=print&p_docid=0F84FAC490039, Aug. 20, 2010.

54 a frustrated Notre Dame defender . . . "It's playbooks.": Tudor, "From the Bag of Tricks."

54 wideout Bryan Peterson, a former . . . for a 3-yard TD run.: Tudor, "From the Bag of Tricks."

188

WOLFPACK

54 When you run trick plays . . . question your sanity.: Bettinger, p. 32.
55 Gabriel chose State over 71 . . . linebackers than signal callers.": "Roman Gabriel," *NC State University Wolfpack: Football*, https://admin.xosn.com/ViewArticle.dbml?DB_OEM_ID=9200&ATCLID=1472712, Aug. 6, 2010.
55 most teams alternated their quarterback: Mumau, p. 71.
55 defensive coordinator Al Michaels . . . into the defensive drills.: Mumau, p. 74.
55 In 1960, with State clinging . . . ran out to the 29.: "Roman Gabriel."
56 "turned the area's admiration . . . a flaming infatuation." Herakovich, p. 32.
56 Prior to the UNC game . . . with rocks and curses.: Herakovich, p. 34.
56 The crowd that night had . . . on the Raleigh campus.: Herakovich, p. 35.
57 T.A. McLendon failed to show up . . . his first career start.: Chip Alexander, "Pack Escapes," *The News & Observer*, Sept. 22, 2002, http://nl.newsbank.com/nl-search/we/Archives?p_action=print&p_docid=0F6379FCDBD, Aug. 19, 2010.
57 who had a surprise pre-game . . . basketball coach Bobby Knight,: Chip Alexander, "Knight Time Followed by Near Nightmare for Pack," *The News & Observer*, Sept. 22, 2002, http://nl.newsbank.com/nl-search/we/Archives?p_action=print&p_docid=0F6379FD19456, Aug. 19, 2010.
57 "Hey, I thought it was over,": Alexander, "Pack Escapes."
58 When Pucillo was an eighth . . . a few college-prep courses.: Peeler, p. 42.
58 Temple had a basketball team, . . . for a 25-1 team.: Peeler, pp. 42-43.
58 State assistant coach Vic Bubas . . . his gregarious personality.: Peeler, p. 43.
58 the smallest player Case ever . . . scholarship at NC State,: Peeler, p. 43.
59 Ritcher wasn't even considering . . . Buckey were present.: Mumau, pp. 167-68.
59 "I really liked them . . . instantly lovely for him": Mumau, p. 168.
59 "It was sort of funny," . . . wanted to play defense.: Mumau, pp. 168-69.
59 At Ritcher's first day of . . . would never have believed it.": Mumau, p. 169.
59 I actually started to like . . . didn't seem too bad.: Mumau, p. 169.
60 the student body rushed . . . had wished it for hers.: Edward G. Robinson III, "Wolfpack Upsets Heels as 'Everything' Works," *The News & Observer*, Feb. 17, 2007.
60 It brought tears to . . . not an emotional person.: Edward G. Robinson III, "Wolfpack Upsets Heels."
61 While he encouraged his . . . "Forget all that crap!": Peeler, p. 10.
61 He took a trip down to . . . can't play against a zone.": Peeler, p. 12.
61 Case requested that he be buried . . . Duke and Wake Forest.: Peeler, p. 12.
62 "it appeared that the old . . . reclaim his throne.": Herakovich, pp. 102-03.
62 "They had the ball . . . something good happen quickly.": Herakovich, p. 103.
62 It wasn't any brainstorm on my part.: Herakovich, p. 103.
63 dubbed the White Shoes Gang by senior linebacker Chuck Amato.: Mumau, p. 65.
63 "the most monumental in the school's history.": Mumau, p. 65.
64 "was the irreplaceable leader . . . our season is over.": Peeler, p. 121.

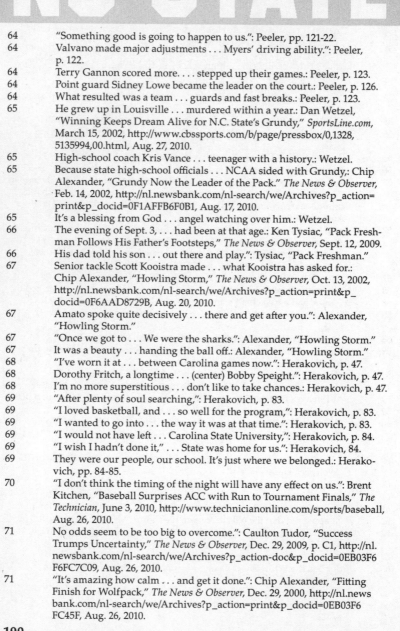
64   "Something good is going to happen to us.": Peeler, pp. 121-22.
64   Valvano made major adjustments . . . Myers' driving ability.": Peeler, p. 122.
64   Terry Gannon scored more. . . . stepped up their games.: Peeler, p. 123.
64   Point guard Sidney Lowe became the leader on the court.: Peeler, p. 126.
64   What resulted was a team . . . guards and fast breaks.: Peeler, p. 123.
65   He grew up in Louisville . . . murdered within a year.: Dan Wetzel, "Winning Keeps Dream Alive for N.C. State's Grundy," SportsLine.com, March 15, 2002, http://www.cbssports.com/b/page/pressbox/0,1328, 5135994,00.html, Aug. 27, 2010.
65   High-school coach Kris Vance . . . teenager with a history.: Wetzel.
65   Because state high-school officials . . . NCAA sided with Grundy,: Chip Alexander, "Grundy Now the Leader of the Pack." The News & Observer, Feb. 14, 2002, http://nl.newsbank.com/nl-search/we/Archives?p_action=print&p_docid=0F1AFFB6F0B1, Aug. 17, 2010.
65   It's a blessing from God . . . angel watching over him.: Wetzel.
66   The evening of Sept. 3, . . . had been at that age.: Ken Tysiac, "Pack Freshman Follows His Father's Footsteps," The News & Observer, Sept. 12, 2009.
66   His dad told his son . . . out there and play.": Tysiac, "Pack Freshman."
67   Senior tackle Scott Kooistra made . . . what Kooistra has asked for.: Chip Alexander, "Howling Storm," The News & Observer, Oct. 13, 2002, http://nl.newsbank.com/nl-search/we/Archives?p_action=print&p_docid=0F6AAD8729B, Aug. 20, 2010.
67   Amato spoke quite decisively . . . there and get after you.": Alexander, "Howling Storm."
67   "Once we got to . . . We were the sharks.": Alexander, "Howling Storm."
67   It was a beauty . . . handing the ball off.: Alexander, "Howling Storm."
68   "I've worn it at . . . between Carolina games now.": Herakovich, p. 47.
68   Dorothy Fritch, a longtime . . . (center) Bobby Speight.": Herakovich, p. 47.
68   I'm no more superstitious . . . don't like to take chances.: Herakovich, p. 47.
69   "After plenty of soul searching,": Herakovich, p. 83.
69   "I loved basketball, and . . . so well for the program,": Herakovich, p. 83.
69   "I wanted to go into . . . the way it was at that time.": Herakovich, p. 83.
69   "I would not have left . . . Carolina State University,": Herakovich, p. 84.
69   "I wish I hadn't done it," . . . State was home for us.": Herakovich, 84.
69   They were our people, our school. It's just where we belonged.: Herakovich, pp. 84-85.
70   "I don't think the timing of the night will have any effect on us.": Brent Kitchen, "Baseball Surprises ACC with Run to Tournament Finals," The Technician, June 3, 2010, http://www.technicianonline.com/sports/baseball, Aug. 26, 2010.
71   No odds seem to be too big to overcome.": Caulton Tudor, "Success Trumps Uncertainty," The News & Observer, Dec. 29, 2009, p. C1, http://nl.newsbank.com/nl-search/we/Archives?p_action-doc&p_docid=0EB03F6 F6FC7C09, Aug. 26, 2010.
71   "It's amazing how calm . . . and get it done.": Chip Alexander, "Fitting Finish for Wolfpack," The News & Observer, Dec. 29, 2000, http://nl.news bank.com/nl-search/we/Archives?p_action=print&p_docid=0EB03F6 FC45F, Aug. 26, 2010.

WOLFPACK

71 "most incredible, improbable comeback yet": Alexander, "Fitting Finish."

71 "That was a little spark,": Alexander, "Fitting Finish."

71 We were down 24-0, . . . not to this team.: Alexander, "Fitting Finish."

72 State's three seniors in . . . high-school all-star games.: Peeler, *When March Went Mad*, p. 194.

72 Cavalier fans taunted State . . . "N-I-T!" "N-I-T!" "N-I-T!": Peeler, *When March Went Mad*, p. 194.

72 "That was ugly," . . . "And God don't like ugly.": Peeler, *When March Went Mad*, p. 195.

72 In the last half, though, . . . around under the baskets.: Peeler, *When March Went Mad*, p. 196.

72 Man, I'd like to pay them back for that in a big way.: Peeler, *When March Went Mad*, p. 168.

73 During the 1922 football season, . . . team as the Wolfpack.: Mumau, p. 35.

73 The basketball team remained . . . squad the "Ted Terrors.": Herakovich, p. 12.

73 In 1946, Chancellor J.W. . . . however, was the Wolfpack.: Mumau, p. 35.

73 The wolf is a scrappy, . . . spttin' image of our team.: Mumau, p. 35.

74 "playing for NC State was . . . to get into a major college.: Peeler, p. 137.

74 an immediate "leader on a team that lacked discipline.": Peeler, p. 138.

74 playing pro ball wasn't even . . . That surprised McMillan,: Peeler, p. 137.

75 Thirty-three alums died . . . delayed the tower's completion.: "Memorial Bell Tower," ncsu.edu, http://www.ncsu.edu/facilities/buildings/tower/html, Aug. 2, 2010.

75 Veterans returning home . . . students' wives or dates.: Herakovich, p. 33.

75 During the 1946-47 season, . . . going toward the tower.: Herakovich, p. 35.

76 "Just another day at the ballpark,": Chip Alexander, "State Can Celebrate," *The News & Observer*, Nov. 11, 2007.

76 In the huddle, . . . to make a play,": Alexander, "State Can Celebrate."

76 Wide receivers Darrell in the fight song.: Alexander, "State Can Celebrate."

76 There's so much joy and excitement.: Alexander, "State Can Celebrate."

77 his father, Press, announced the birth . . . was always around basketball.": Mark Kriegel, "The Pistol," *Sports Illustrated*, Jan. 8, 2007, http://sportsillustrated.cnn.com/vault/article/magazine/MAG1116086, Nov. 1, 2009.

77 When he was the head . . . what they called "Showtime.": Kriegel.

77 the son couldn't make the SAT scores required to matriculate at State.: Peeler, p. 65.

78 For two and a half years, . . . guard spots for the Wolfpack.: Peeler, *Legends of N.C. State Basketball*, p. 144.

78 "There is no question that frustration set in,": Peeler, *Legends of N.C. State Basketball*, p. 145.

78 "My father told me, . . . the coach will play you.'": Peeler, *Legends of N.C. State Basketball*, p. 145.

78 was a two-time junior college . . . being benched by quitting.: Peeler, *Legends of N.C. State Basketball*, p. 144.

78 His son may have had . . . Del Negro's first two seasons.: Peeler, *Legends of N.C. State Basketball*, p. 145.

78 I let frustration creep in . . . opportunity to play would

come.: Peeler, *Legends of N.C. State Basketball*, p. 145.

79   Growing up, DiNardo dreamed of playing . . . as his father, Phil, had.: Peeler, *When March Went Mad*, p. 176.

79   When no major schools . . . dream of playing ball for State.: Peeler, *When March Went Mad*, p. 177.

79   The fast friends transferred . . . working on his engineering degree: Peeler, *When March Went Mad*, p. 178.

79   Coach Jim Valvano announced . . . what size shoes he wore.: Peeler, *When March Went Mad*, p. 179.

79   "Tommy was an important part of our team,": Peeler, *When March Went Mad*, p. 180.

79   It kind of hit me that my dream was coming true.: Peeler, *When March Went Mad*, p. 179.

80   He knew the home crowd . . . short time to get there.: Chip Alexander, "Mad 'Dash' Lifts Wolfpack," *The News & Observer*, Oct 12, 2003, http://nl.newsbank.com/nl-search/we/Archives?p_action=print&p_docid=0FE24A5AC95A, Aug. 20, 2010.

80   he later called "a dumb pick.": Alexander, "Mad 'Dash.'"

80   He first ran to his . . . grabbed him at the 1,: Alexander, "Mad 'Dash.'"

81   *USA Today* called the greatest fullback in Wolfpack history,: Bob Boyles and Paul Guido, *The USA Today College Football Encyclopedia 2009-10* (New York City: Skyhorse Publishing, Inc., 2009), p. 1130.

81   was his 36th, a new conference record: Mumau, p. 121.

82   crowd of 12,400 on a snowy night: Chip Alexander, "Grant Steals One for the Pack," *The News & Observer*, Jan. 20, 2008.

82   "I saw J.J. make . . . and we can win,": Alexander, "Grant Steals One."

82   He threw it right . . . I was like, 'Thanks.': Alexander, "Grant Steals One."

83   "I have been fortunate in my investments,": Peeler, *Legends of N.C. State Basketball*, p. 4

83   believing that his not . . . would embarrass the school.: Peeler, *Legends of N.C. State Basketball*, p. 4.

83   While he was coaching high . . . Both ventures were successful.: Peeler, *Legends of N.C. State Basketball*, p. 8.

83   He often tipped his players . . . stock broker downtown.: Peeler, *Legends of N.C. State Basketball*, p. 8.

83   In 1959, he sought to bring . . . "Everett Case's McDonald's.": Peeler, *Legends of N.C. State Basketball*, pp. 8-9.

83   Case left an estate of . . . It was a godsend.": Peeler, *Legends of N.C. State Basketball*, p. 7.

84   "without question . . . the most . . . Wolfpack basketball program": Herakovich, p. 101.

84   Thompson's foot caught the shoulder . . . perpendicular to his body.: Peeler, *Legends of N.C. State Basketball*, p. 83.

84   He lay unconscious . . . a devastating head injury.": Peeler, *Legends of N.C. State Basketball*, p. 82.

84   When teammate Tommy Burleson . . . got physically ill.: Peeler, *Legends of N.C. State Basketball*, p. 83.

84   "a soft-spoken, polite-as-a-preacher young man who never got angry.: Peeler, *Legends of N.C. State Basketball*, p. 82.

84   The officials let Pitt slap . . . to block the next Pitt shot.: Peeler, *Legends of N.C. State Basketball*, p. 83.

84   "I got a little upset," . . . I paid a huge price for it,": Peeler, *Legends of N.C. State Basketball*, p. 83.

84   "a purely selfish matter and . . . unwelcome misfortune or frustration": Bruce T. Dahlberg, "Anger," *The Interpreter's Dictionary of the Bible* (Nashville: Abingdon Press, 1962), Vol. 1, p. 136.

84   That was a reckless act . . . on the basketball court.: Peeler, *Legends of N.C. State Basketball*, p. 83.

85   "I jumped over the end," . . . wearing a face mask.: A.J. Carr, "Memories from Half-Century Ago," *The News & Observer*, Oct. 12, 2002, http://nl. newsbank.com/nl-search/we/Archives?p_action=print&p_docid= 0F6A265E84F6, Aug. 20, 2010.

85   with the quarterback, co-captain . . . scored virtually untouched: Douglas Herakovich quoted in "Wolfpack Football Through the Decades," *Section Six*, July 24, 2007, http://sectionsixblogsport.com/2007/07/wolfpack-football-through-decades.html, Aug. 20, 2010.

85   It was the highlight of the year. The whole student body went crazy.: Carr, "Memories from Half-Century Ago."

86   a storybook finish, an unforgettable . . . making his first college start.: Chip Alexander, "Pack Grabs Big Win," *The News & Observer*, Sept. 24, 2006.

86   Looking like a fifth-year senior,: Alexander, "Pack Grabs Big Win."

86   Evan pump-faked and moved . . . as he hit the turf.": Alexander. "Pack Grabs Big Win."

86   "It's an amazing feeling," . . . is just amazing.": Alexander, "Pack Grabs Big Win."

86   They never stopped believing.: Alexander, "Pack Grabs Big Win."

87   As the last timeout ended, . . . get a dunk to win the game.": Phillip Lee, "Classic Catches Up with Lorenzo Charles," *ESPN Classic*, Nov. 19, 2003, http://espn.go.com/classic/s/Where_now_Charles_Lorenzo.html, Aug. 5, 2010.

87   Charles "used to try to . . . he tried to dunk him.": Peeler, *Legends of N.C. State Basketball*, p. 132.

87   As he saw little action . . . broke a foot in January,: Peeler, *Legends of N.C. State Basketball*, p. 131.

87   "There were times when he couldn't run . . . their sons guard him.: Peeler, *Legends of N.C. State Basketball*, p. 132.

87   More than 20 years later, . . . and that would be it.: Peeler, *Legends of N.C. State Basketball*, p. 131.

88   "a big surprise for everybody, including Williford.": Peeler, *Legends of N.C. State Basketball*, p. 66.

88   Williford dreamed of playing . . . overlook the 6'6" forward.: *Legends of N.C. State Basketball*, Peeler, p. 64.

88   He committed to Pfeiffer . . . he got a better offer.: *Legends of N.C. State Basketball*, Peeler, p. 65.

88   Press Maravich had no interest . . . to the 1966-67 season.: *Legends of N.C. State Basketball*, Peeler, pp. 64-65.

88   When new head coach . . . offered Willford a scholarship.: *Legends of N.C. State Basketball*, Peeler, p. 65.

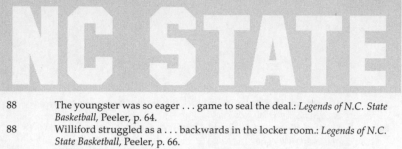

BIBLIOGRAPHY

Alexander, Chip. "An Oh-So-Sweet Sunday." *The News & Observer*. 21 March 2005. htttp://nl.newsbank.com/nl-search/we/Archives?p_action=print&p_docid=108FC9A484ED.

---. "Fitting Finish for Wolfpack: Big State Rally Stuns Gophers." *The News & Observer*. 29 Dec. 2000. http://nl.newsbank.com/nl-search/we/Archives?p_action=print&p_docid=0EB03F6FC45F.

---. "Grant Steals One for the Pack: State Gets Victory over Miami in OT." *The News & Observer*. 20 Jan. 2008.

---. "Grundy Now the Leader of the Pack." *The News & Observer*. 14 Feb. 2002. http://nl.newsbank.com/nl-search/we/Archives?p_action=print&p_docid=0F1AFFB6F0B1.

---. "Howling Storm." *The News & Observer*. 13 Oct. 2002. http://nl.newsbank.com/nl-search/we/Archives?p_action=print&p=docid=0F6AAD8769B.

---. "Knight Time Followed by Near Nightmare for Pack." *The News & Observer*. 22 Sept. 2002. http://nl.newsbank.com/nl-search/we/Archives?p_action=print&p_docid=0F6379FD19456.

---. "Lowe and Behold: First-Year NCSU Coach Sidney Lowe and His Pack Stun No. 3 Heels." *The News & Observer*. 4 Feb. 2007.

---. "Mad 'Dash' Lifts Wolfpack." *The News & Observer*. 12 Oct. 2003. http://nl.news bank.com/nl-search/we/Archives?p_action=print&p_docid=0FE24A5AC95A.

---. "O'Brien's Approach: Keep It Simple, State." *The News & Observer*. 10 Aug. 2007.

---. "Pack Escapes." *The News & Observer*. 22 Sept. 2002. http://nl.newsbank.com/nl-search/we/Archives?p_action=print&p_docid=0F6379FCDBD.

---. "Pack Grabs Big Win: In His First Start, QB Daniel Evans Shows Poise While leading State to the TD in the Final Minute." *The News & Observer*. 24 Sept. 2006.

---. "Postgame Report." *The News & Observer*. 3 Oct. 2004. http://nl.newsbank.com/nl-search/we/Archives?p_action=print&p_docid=1057F4780EE54.

---. "State Can Celebrate: In Another Classic Matchup Between the Rivals, NCSU Uses a Late Touchdown and a Defensive Stand to Knock Off UNC." *The News*

194

& Observer. 11 Nov. 2007.

---. "The Pack Is Back." *The News & Observer.* 10 March 2002. http://nl.newsbank.com/
nl-search/we/Archives?p_action=print&p_docid=0F22F913056B7.

---. "Throwing His Own Way." *The News & Observer.* 24 Aug. 2002. http://nl.news
bank.com/nl-search/we/Archives?p_action=print&p_docid=0F59F999A38A.

---. "'We Make Games Exciting': McCauley's Slam Downs Deacons." *The News &
Observer.* 4 Feb. 2008.

Bettinger, Jim & Julie S. *The Book of Bowden.* Nashville: TowleHouse Publishing, 2001.

Boyles, Bob and Paul Guido. *The USA Today College Football Encyclopedia 2009-10.* New
York City: Skyhorse Publishing, Inc., 2009.

Cairns, Bob. *V & Me: Everybody's Favorite Jim Valvano Story.* Alexander, NC: Alexander
Books, 2005.

Carr, A.J. "'74 Players Sing Each Other's Praises: Thompson Says Stoddard Was
Glue." *The News & Observer.* 23 Dec. 2008.

---. "College Tennis' Greatest Match." *gopack.com.* 31 July 2010. http://www.gopack.
com/sports/m-tennis/spec-rel/073110aaa.html.

---. "Heart of a Champion: Wolfpack's Darrion Caldwell Withstands Outside Pres-
sures, Stays the Course and Claims NCAA Wrestling Championship." *The
News & Observer.* 29 March 2009.

---. "Memories from Half-Century Ago." *The News & Observer.* 12 Oct. 2002. http://nl.
newsbank.com/nl-search/we/Archives?p_action=print&p_docid=0F6A265
E84F6.

---. "'She's in a Better Place': Admirers of Kay Yow Pay Their Respects to a Woman
Who Touched So Many." *The News & Observer.* 25 Jan. 2009.

---. "The Pack is Back." *The News & Observer.* 10 March 2002. C1. http://nl.newsbank.
com/nl-search/we/Archives?p_action=print&p_docid=0F22F913056B7.

Carter, Rachel. "State's Strong Arm: ACC Player of the Year Abbie Sims Scorches Foes
with Speed, Movement." *The News & Observer.* 10 May 2007.

"A Coach's First Season: Q&A with Kellie Harper." *gopack.com.* 6 April 2010. http://
www.gopack.com/sports/w-baskbl/spec-rel/040610aaa.html.

Dahlberg, Bruce T. "Anger." *The Interpreter's Dictionary of the Bible.* Nashville: Abingdon Press, 1962. Vol. 1. 135-37.

Dinich, Heather. "Irving Won't Be Limited in Practice." *ESPN.com.* 26 Feb. 2010. http://
sports.espn.go.com/ncf/news/story?id=4948979.

Giglio, J.P. "State's Sure Shot." *The News & Observer.* 20 Jan. 2010.

Henry, Jim. "N.C. State's Nate Irving Thankful for Second Chance -- at Life and Football." *fanhouse.com.* 6 July 2010. http://ncaafootball.fanhouse.com/2010/07/06.

Herakovich, Douglas. *Wolfpack Handbook: Stories, Stats and Stuff about N.C. State Basketball.* Wichita, KS: The Wichita Eagle and Beacon Publishing Co., 1996.

---. Quoted in "Wolfpack Football Through the Decades." *Section Six.* 24 July 2007.
http://sectionsixblogspot.com/2007/07/wolfpack-football-through-decades.
html.

Kitchen, Brent. "Baseball Surprises ACC with Run to Tournament Finals." *The Technician.* 3 June 2010. http://www.technicianonline.com/sports/baseball.

Kriegel, Mark. "The Pistol." *Sports Illustrated.* 8 Jan. 2007. http://sportsillustrated.cnn.
com/vault/article/magazine/MAG1116086.

Lee, Phillip. "Classic Catches Up with Lorenzo Charles." *ESPN Classic.* 19 Nov.
2003. http://espn.go.com/classic/s/Where_now_charles_lorenzo
html.

MacArthur, John. *Twelve Ordinary Men*. Nashville: W Publishing Group, 2002.

"Memorial Bell Tower." *ncsu.edu*. http://www.ncsu.edu/facilities/buildings/tower/ html.

Mumau, Thad. *Go Wolfpack! North Carolina State Football*. Huntsville, AL: The Strode Publishers, 1981.

Myatt, Al. "Finally, a Real Home Game." *The News & Observer*. 2 April 2003. http:/ /nl.newsbank.com/nl-search/we/Archives?p_action=print&p_docid=0FA2B0 D85C04.

Peeler, Tim. "Intense Workouts Prepares [sic] Women's Basketball for Upcoming Season." *gopack.com*. 9 Aug. 2010. http://www.gopack.com/sports/w-baskbl/ spec-rel/080910aae.html.

———. *Legends of N.C. State Basketball*. Champaign, IL: Sports Publishing L.L.C., 2004.

———. *When March Went Mad: A Celebration of NC State's 1982-83 National Championship*. Champaign, IL: Sports Publishing L.L.C., 2007.

Perez, Lorenzo. "After Baby-Sitting, Two-a-Days Not So Daunting: Pack's Harris Will Anchor the Line." *The News & Observer*. 16 July 2006.

Pickeral, Robbi. "Mock Went Both Ways in Rivalry: World War II Veteran Led N.C. State, North Carolina." *The News & Observer*. 10 March 2009.

Robinson, Edward G. III. "Harpers Are a Coaching Marriage." *The News & Observer*. 3 March 2010.

———. "Wolfpack Upsets Heels as 'Everything' Works." *The News & Observer*. 17 Feb. 2007.

"Roman Gabriel." *NC State University Wolfpack: Football*. https://admin.xosn.com/ ViewArticle.dbml?DB_OEM_ID=9200&ATCLID=1472712.

Sumner, Jim. "Looking Back: NC State's Legendary ACC Tournament Title." *TheACC.com*. 7 March 2007. http://www.theacc.com/sports/m-baskbl/spec- rel/030707aaf.html.

———. "Looking Back: NC State's Road to Omaha 40 Years Ago." *TheACC.com*. 30 April 2008. http://www.theacc.com/sports/m-basebl/spec-rel/043008aaa.html.

———. "Looking Back: The 1957 NC State Football Team's Run to the ACC Crown." *TheACC. com*. 10 Oct. 2007. http://www.theacc.com/sports/m-footbl/spec-rel/101007aaa.html.

Taylor, John. "It's a Miracle NC State LB Nate Irving Is Still Amongst the Living." *nbcsports.com*. 25 July 2010. http://collegefootballtalk.nbcsports.com/2010/07/25.

Tudor, Caulton. "Davis Heats Up Just in Time to Save Pack's Day." *The News & Observer*. 3 Oct. 2004. http://nl.newsbank.com/nl-search/we/Archives?p_ action=print&p_docid=1057F477FB889.

———. "From the Bag of Tricks." *The News & Observer*. 2 Jan. 2003. http://nl.newsbank. com/nl-search/we/Archives?p_action=print&p_docid=0F84FAC490039.

———. "Success Trumps Uncertainty." *The News & Observer*. 29 Dec. 2000. C1. http://nl. newsbank.com/nl-search/we/Archives?p_action=doc&p_docid=0EB03F6 FC7C09.

Tysiac, Ken. "Pack Freshman Follows His Father's Footsteps." *The News & Observer*. 12 Sept. 2009.

Voepel, Mechelle. "Yow's Considerable Efforts Will Live On." *ESPN.com*. 24 Jan. 2009. http://sports.espn.go.com/ncw/columns/story?columnist=voepel_ mechelle&id=3853652.

Wetzel, Dan. "Winning Keeps Dream Alive for N.C. State's Grundy." *SportsLine.com*. 15 March 2002. http://www.cbssports.com/b/page/pressbox/0,1328,5135994,00. html.

WOLFPACK

INDEX
(LAST NAME, DEVOTION DAY NUMBER)

197